WHAT PRICE **PACS?**

WHAT PRICE **PACS?**

Report of the
Twentieth Century Fund
Task Force on
Political Action Committees

Background Paper
by Frank J. Sorauf

The Twentieth Century Fund/New York/1984

FOREWORD

The financing of political campaigning in the United States has long been a source of concern. Most Americans want fair and hard-fought election contests between the best possible candidates. We do not want our politics to become the preserve of the rich or of special interests. At the same time, we believe that every viewpoint ought to get at least a hearing.

The trouble is that politics can never be as fair and evenhanded as we would like it to be. Money talks in politics, the advantages of incumbency cannot be easily offset, and the costs of new technologies, especially television but also computers, continue to rise. The result is that, despite a measure of public financing for presidential elections and rules calling for financial disclosure by candidates, public distrust and skepticism about the fairness of our politics is widespread.

This skepticism and even cynicism has grown with the increasing cost of political campaigns and the rapid rise to prominence of political action committees (PACs). Although they have been around for some time, PACs really attained significance only in the last general election. As an important new political force—and a growing source of dollars for politics—there have been calls for limiting their power and influence. Thus, the Twentieth Century Fund, which has long had an active research program on campaign finance, decided to seek a balanced appraisal of the role of PACs. We asked Frank J. Sorauf, professor of political science at the University of Minnesota and an authority on PACs, to prepare a comprehensive background paper on their growth and role, and then assembled an independent Task Force to consider what to do about them.

The Task Force was tantamount to a brain trust on campaign finance. It included veterans of the political wars from each of the major parties who have witnessed—and had to accommodate to—many changes in the patterns of campaign financing, fund raising,

v

176214

lobbying, and campaigning over the past five decades. It was a diverse, knowledgeable, and involved group. Many have raised money for campaigns; some managed PACs; some were active long before the passage of the Federal Election Campaign Act, while others have operated only since the Federal Election Commission (FEC) set down the rules regulating campaign finance.

Given their diversity, it is not surprising that their deliberations were marked by sharp disagreements, and that their divisions are reflected in the Comments and Dissents that follow the Report of the majority. But it must also be noted that the Task Force reached a consensus on a number of points. It agreed that the tenor of our election campaigns has deteriorated as a result of the activities of those PACs that engage in independent expenditures; the entire Task Force criticized the lack of accountability of such PACs to the electorate and condemned the shrill invective they have frequently injected into campaigns. But here, as elsewhere, the recommendations of the Task Force were constrained by the Supreme Court's decision in *Buckley v. Valeo*. Still, there was general agreement on some incremental steps to restore a greater measure of civility and integrity to campaigning.

The Task Force also reached agreement on the need for mechanisms to build broad coalitions out of fragmented and diverse interests, and took the view that our existing political parties were the preferred mechanism. The Task Force unanimously recommended raising the limits on individual contributions to parties, party contributions to candidates, and party spending in publicly funded presidential campaigns.

As can readily be imagined, it was no easy task to moderate the discussions of so committed a group. Senator Muskie exhibited his parliamentary skills and his diplomatic ability in chairing the meetings; Charls Walker was an astute and able vice-chairman, particularly adept, even in dissent, at seeking out areas of agreement and common concern. A special debt is owed to Frank Sorauf, who placed the recent growth of PACs in the broader perspective of changing campaign technology, voter behavior, and party decline. I must also make mention of the guest witnesses who offered their insights and views: Reps. Dan Glickman (D.-Kan.) and William Thomas (R.-Cal.); Lee Ann Elliott and Thomas Harris, both of the FEC; Bernadette Budde (BIPAC); Victor Kamber (PROPAC); Peter Lauer (AMPAC); Stephen Conafay, Pfizer Inc.; and Paul Weyrich, Committee for the Survival of a Free Congress. We are grateful to each of them.

We especially appreciate the effort made by the Task Force to confront the problems posed by PACs. It has produced a careful and balanced evaluation, which should allay some of the fears about PACs while making clear that some of the concerns are justified. In doing so, it has laid the groundwork for a more informed debate over what to do about PACs.

M. J. Rossant, *Director*
TWENTIETH CENTURY FUND
December 1983

CONTENTS

TASK FORCE MEMBERS

Edmund S. Muskie, *chairman*
Senior Partner, Chadbourne, Parke, Whiteside & Wolff; formerly, Secretary of State and U.S. Senator from Maine

Herbert Alexander
Director, Citizens' Research Foundation and Professor of Political Science, University of Southern California

Yvonne Brathwaite Burke
Counsel, Fine, Perzik & Friedman, Los Angeles; formerly, U.S. Representative from California

John C. Culver
Partner, Arent, Fox, Kintner, Plotkin & Kahn, Washington, D.C.; formerly, U.S. Senator from Iowa

John W. Gray, Jr.
Assistant Vice-President and Attorney, American Telephone & Telegraph Co., Washington, D.C.

Terry Herndon
President, Citizens Against Nuclear War, Washington, D.C.; formerly, Executive Director, National Education Association, Washington, D.C.

William J. Holayter
Director, Legislative and Political Action Department, International Association of Machinists and Aerospace Workers, Washington, D.C.

Arthur B. Krim
Chairman, Orion Pictures Corporation, New York; formerly, Finance Chairman, Democratic National Committee

John A. Love
Chairman and Chief Executive Officer, Ideal Basic Industries, Denver; formerly, Governor of Colorado

Robert Price
President, Price Communications Corporation, New York; formerly, Deputy Mayor of New York

James Rowe
Partner, Corcoran, Youngman & Rowe, Washington, D.C.

Richard Thaxton
Vice-President in Charge of Political Affairs, National Association of Realtors, Washington, D.C.

Charls E. Walker
Chairman, Charls E. Walker Associates, Washington, D.C.; formerly, Deputy Secretary of the Treasury

Frank Sorauf, *rapporteur*
Professor of Political Science, University of Minnesota

Report of the Task Force

The rapid growth of political action committees (PACs) has been a mounting source of concern and apprehension for many Americans. The role of PACs in campaign finance is now so pervasive, and the attention they receive so extensive, that they have become the centerpiece of a new devil theory of American politics. This Task Force deplores the emotionalism and the sensationalism that often accompany discussion of PACs. Yet we recognize that public concern is rooted in the unsettling revolution that has taken place in campaign finance.

PACs are now the quintessential organizations of the new campaign politics, the chief conduit for channeling money from business, labor unions, professional associations, and other groups to candidates seeking public office. Statistics tell much of the tale:

• In 1974, there were 608 PACs registered with the Federal Election Commission (FEC); at the time of the 1982 congressional elections, the number of PACs had jumped to nearly 3,400.

• PACs contributed $12.5 million to candidates for the House and Senate in 1974; contributions climbed to $80 million in 1982.

• PAC contributions amounted to 13 percent of congressional candidates' campaign receipts in 1974; that figure reached 27 percent in 1982.

All signs suggest that PAC growth at the state level, which is not reported to the FEC, has soared as high and as rapidly.

Because PACs have become so numerous and appear so powerful, their opponents use them as convenient scapegoats for many of the ills afflicting our politics, charging them with doing more damage than they could possibly do. PACs are, after all, only one funding source, admittedly the fastest-growing source, in our complex system for financing political campaigns. But what makes PACs so controversial and so convenient a scapegoat is that the money they contribute is so closely linked to a specific cause or special interest.

It must be remembered that the expression of specific group interests is not only a deep-rooted tradition but also a legal and proper exercise of constitutional rights, a safeguard against governmental tyranny. In a political system dedicated to majority rule, it is imperative that minorities be heard. PACs provide a means of expression for many different interest groups in our large and heterogeneous society, giving voice to the beliefs and objectives of millions of Americans who might otherwise have difficulty in making known their views. Without them, our society's pluralistic richness and the vigor of our politics would be diminished. Whatever our individual differences about PACs—and this Task Force has had some sharp disagreements—we unanimously believe that PACs have a legitimate place in American politics.

Nevertheless, a majority of the Task Force sees a simple reason to be disturbed by the unbridled proliferation of PACs. We are especially dismayed by their ability, real and potential, to furnish campaign contributions in return for legislative influence.

Undue Influence?

At a time of escalating campaign costs, many Americans harbor the suspicion that the sizable contributions funneled to politicians through PACs demand a quid pro quo. A democratic polity that rests upon respect for the political system and its officeholders cannot afford even the appearance of influence peddling. Although we do not think that money is swapped for votes in any crude or overt way by these PACs, they are able to secure privileged access to elected officials and to command special attention to particular issues. This form of influence is a matter of serious concern. At the very least, it sets up a moral dilemma for congressmen, who find themselves in the compromising position of soliciting funds from the very individuals and groups that are desirous of swaying their votes. The resulting appearance of unsavory compromise diminishes respect for those who seek or hold office and thereby presents a threat to our democratic system.

There is also the danger that PACs may be used by corporations, unions, or associations to win undue political influence. Many interest groups now magnify their legislative influence by lobbying on their own behalf and simultaneously setting up PACs to handle campaign contributions and to engage in related political activity. Under federal statutes, parent organizations can pay the administrative costs of their PACs and closely control and manage their governance. Consistently, analyses of PAC spending reveal a single-minded pursuit of legislative agendas.

To some extent, the political power achieved by PACs is the by-product of past reforms in campaign financing. But even though there are serious flaws in present election arrangements, we see much to applaud in the existing structure of federal regulation of campaign finance; the limits on contributions, the reporting and disclosure requirements, the tax credits for political contributions, and the independent oversight and administration by the FEC. Critics point out that, in real terms, inflation has "lowered" the contribution limits set in the early 1970s, but, in light of the growth in campaign funding available to candidates, we would not raise most existing limits. As for disclosure requirements, we consider them an effective means of achieving accountability. Given the amount of information on spending and receipts now registered with the FEC—far more, in all likelihood, than either the commission or the media can readily digest—it would be, we feel, a mistake to add to current reporting requirements.

It is our view that PACs are but one aspect of a bigger problem: our system of financing political campaigns. Reform of campaign financing has often had unintended consequences. Certainly, the controversy now surrounding PACs can be traced to the unintended side effects of past reforms.

PACs have been around for some time, dating back to the labor movement during World War II. But their spectacular ascendancy did not begin until the 1970s, when post-Watergate campaign finance regulation placed stringent limits on individual contributions to candidates while placing higher limits on PAC contributions, thus enhancing their prestige. In retrospect, the subsequent flow of money was predictable, though not fully foreseen. In addition, the adoption of public funding for presidential campaigns served to accelerate the growth of PACs; funds that had once gone to committees for presidential candidates were now given to the political committees of congressional candidates.

Buckley v. Valeo

An even more significant stimulus to the rapid expansion of PAC influence was the Supreme Court's 1976 decision in *Buckley v. Valeo.* That decision struck down limits on the sums that candidates could spend, the use of personal fortunes by candidates, and independent spending by groups and individuals in campaigns, all of which had been imposed by congressional amendments to the Federal Election Campaign Act in 1974. Whatever the merits of the Supreme Court decision—based on every citizen's constitutionally guaranteed freedom to engage in political activity—the effect has been to foster unrestricted growth of campaign costs and to increase the potential for the abuse of PACs in campaign financing.

This Task Force does not believe that our politics ought to invite charges that we get the best candidates money can buy. On the contrary, we think that American politics will be enhanced by lessening the role of money and by ensuring the integrity—and the appearance of integrity—of candidates for public office. In considering how best to attain these ends, a large majority of us have concluded that the *Buckley* decision was wrongheaded. It has triggered unrestrained growth in campaign costs. It has, moreover, severely limited the options available to Congress for curbing or controlling that growth.

We believe that the Supreme Court, which has recognized Congress's legitimate interest in legislating against corruption, must give Congress the legal authority to enact measures to limit campaign expenditures. So long as *Buckley* stands, however, the power of Congress is restricted. Our own deliberations were circumscribed by *Buckley*; we had no alternative but to consider options that met the Court's present test of constitutionality.

With this caveat in mind, *the Task Force urges Congress to enact legislation limiting the total amount of money that candidates can receive from PACs in a campaign period.* We endorse proposals that would hold PAC contributions to a House candidate below $100,000; PAC contributions to a candidate for the Senate would necessarily be higher because of the greater scope and costs of senatorial campaigns.

Independent Expenditures

A highly questionable funding device—used by some PACs, but also by individuals and groups—is the independent expenditure; that is, an expenditure made expressly to further the election or defeat of a candidate, but made without the knowledge or consent of the candidate, the candidate's committee, or a party committee. In the aftermath of *Buckley*, which abolished limits on such spending, independent expenditures in support of, or in opposition to, candidates have grown even faster than the direct contributions to candidates made by PACs.

In the 1980 presidential election, for example, $13.8 million was spent independently—a figure at least six or seven times greater than independent expenditures in 1976. In the 1980 congressional elections, independent expenditures totaled $2.4 million; that figure jumped to $5.7 million in 1982. Well over 90 percent of these independent expenditures were made by PACs.

The entire Task Force found the absence of public accountability for these independent expenditures particularly distressing. When money is contributed directly to candidates, the candidates must take responsibility for the way it is spent, and watchful voters can reinforce the fact that they must take that responsibility at the polls. With independent expenditures, no such corrective mechanism exists. The bulk of such spending is made by a small number of unaffiliated, ideological PACs that have no parent organization—such as unions, corporations, or trade and professional associations—and that solicit the public primarily through direct-mail appeals. With no sponsoring organization to accept responsibility, and with contributors scattered across the country, those who direct independent expenditures may be tempted to engage in activities that verge on excess. A number have succumbed to this temptation.

In congressional campaigns, independent expenditures are more likely to be used to assail rather than to support candidates. In 1982, for example, the sums spent in opposition to particular congressional candidates were nearly four times those spent on behalf of certain candidates. With considerable frequency, PACs making independent expenditures have resorted to invective and ad hominem attacks that serve only to debase the American political process. Candidates tarred in this manner find it time-consuming and expensive to rebut the charges; even the candidates purportedly helped may be victimized by such tactics.

The growing problem of independent expenditures has no easy solution. In the absence of a Supreme Court reappraisal of Congress's power to limit these expenditures, perhaps the only option is a combination of incremental reforms. *This Task Force recommends that, in the interests of preserving political integrity, Congress strengthen its safeguards to prevent collusion between candidates and those making independent expenditures.* This can be accomplished by tightening the legal definitions of "independence" and "collusion," and by requiring more stringent proofs of independence. In addition, some of us would make some statutory provision for free media time to enable candidates who have been the targets of scurrilous attacks to answer such allegations.

Beyond legislation, the solution may lie in the awareness and sense of fair play of the American electorate. After the conspicuous misfiring of some well-publicized negative campaigns in 1982, that reliance would seem to be well placed.

The Rising Costs of Campaign Politics

The fundamental changes that have taken place in political campaigns have produced an uncontrolled, upward spiral in campaign contributions and expenditures. PACs are both cause and symptom of this costly new style of running for office. If PACs have pumped more money into campaigns, it is partly because more money is required. The rising costs of campaigning for Congress is an especially troubling development. Just from 1980 to 1982, sums spent by candidates for Congress rose by about 48 percent. While inflation can explain some of the increased expenditure, it can by no means account for all of it.

The single most significant cause for rising campaign costs is progressively greater reliance on mass media campaigning for both the Senate and the House. Advances in electronic technology, abetted by sophisticated new techniques of polling, advertising, public relations, and direct mail, have created a slick new form of electioneering. At the same time, the power of political parties—which traditionally recruited campaign labor and resources to produce the votes—has declined. Despite the time, money, and energy contributed by party regulars, our major political parties no longer command the broad loyalties they once enjoyed.

Today's voters, who are better educated and better informed than previous generations, shy away from party affiliations, preferring to pick and choose among candidates and to respond selectively to political issues. As a result, once candidates have amassed sufficient funds, they can hire professionals to run their campaigns, which depend on polling, advertising, and direct mail instead of on precinct workers and ward heelers. The old barter system of party-dominated campaigns—in which volunteers exchanged their labor for favors, access, patronage—has been replaced by a cash-based system of candidate-centered campaigns.

The consequent need of candidates to raise ever-increasing sums of money traps them in a feverish, often nonstop, search for contributions. The funding quest extends beyond election day, as candidates hustle to pay off campaign debts, then build up their war chests for the next campaign. In this climate, a premium is placed on personal riches, and this threatens to bar many Americans from ever competing for public office. It also sets up a dependence on contributors, including PACs, which provide substantial support for incumbent representatives and senators.

Partial Public Funding

In weighing the advantages and disadvantages of PACs as a funding source in American campaign finance, alternative sources of money—public financing, individual contributions, party spending, and the personal wealth of candidates themselves—must be considered. Having pondered this array, *the Task Force recommends that Congress adopt a voluntary program of partial public funding for candidates for Congress.* This money would be available, on a matching basis, to those candidates who raise specified sums from individual contributors. While endorsing the imposition of spending limits, we recommend making more public money available to those candidates whose opponents elect *not* to accept public funding.

We recognize that this recommendation presents a multitude of problems in the present political climate. Faced with substantial federal deficits and cuts in social programs, the public will be critical of adding public subsidies to already-bloated campaign funds. Members of Congress will find any enactment of public funding for their own campaigns as politically risky as their voting to increase their own salaries. Some incumbents will oppose this measure because they believe the present system works to their advantage. And the potential difficulty of administering funds for hundreds of individual congressional elections is obvious.

But while reform will not come easily in this area, its goal—the restoration of equity to the system of campaign finance—is critical to the well-being of our polity. To those worried about the necessary bureaucratic machinery, we point out that the government already administers tax and regulatory programs of infinitely greater complexity. We are convinced that partial public funding would provide an alternative source of campaign money for candidates with limited personal resources or candidates spurned by PACs; the imbalance between special interests and small contributors thereby would be brought into equilibrium. As a means of safeguarding candidates from suggestions of moral compromise and freeing them from the distracting, time-consuming treadmill of constant fundraising, it is worth the commitment of scarce government resources. What is more, the *Buckley* decision makes such a program the only realistic means of putting a ceiling on campaign expenditures.

Strengthening the Political Parties

The growth of PACs has coincided with, and, alas, contributed to, the decline of political parties and the fragmentation of American politics. Such causality should not be overstated, nor should PACs be blamed for all the changes in political campaigning that concern us. In great measure, the decline of parties and the rise of PACs are reflections of changes in the American electorate, in our society, and in the technological means of campaigning. Nevertheless, PACs, however legitimate, are not a substitute for political parties and cannot match their past contributions to our political system.

Even as political parties are waning in strength, there has emerged a fresh appreciation of their role in the electoral process. Through their recognizable labels and symbols, they give structure and visibility to the options open to voters, enabling them to better distinguish among candidates and their policies as well as to hold politicians accountable once they take office.

As a result of nearly a century of reforms, American political parties are more responsive to citizens than ever before. Even the nomination of candidates has become the province of a wide circle of party activists. Further, political parties are now accountable to their members to a degree unmatched by other political organizations. In contrast, members of most PACs or interest groups have only intermittent dealings with, and indirect control over, their operations. Few PACs, for example, permit contributors a voice in the selection of officials or in the allocation of funds.

For these reasons, and also to introduce more openness and efficiency into the funding process, the Task Force urges a strengthening of the role of political parties in campaign finance. We want to tilt the balance away from the new "functional" politics, dominated by interest groups, and toward the more traditional, constituency-based electoral politics controlled by the parties. The need for this reversal grows more critical as the persistent fragmentation of American politics worsens.

Building Broad Coalitions

Whatever their imperfections as vehicles of majority rule, political parties have been the greatest force behind broad coalitions of support and consent, which is to say, legitimacy. Not only do PACs and interest groups, by definition, fail to attend to the larger public good, but they also limit the vision of many Americans, focusing their attention on a narrow—and often distorted—agenda of issues.

This Task Force believes that America desperately needs stronger mechanisms for building political majorities. In a country of such breadth and diversity, with institutions designed to disperse governmental authority, majority building is inevitably problematic. Even in their heyday, the two major parties had difficulty assembling majorities for programs and policies. In contrast to the party discipline in the British Parliament, the American Congress has performed with a far lower level of party loyalty and cohesion.

In the last analysis, this nation must be able to subordinate specific group interests to the public weal. Otherwise we face either political deadlock or capitulation to a shifting constellation of parochial concerns; these options would breed disenchantment with politicians and politics. *To strengthen our political parties and their capacity for coalition building, this Task Force unanimously recommends that Congress amend the Federal Election Campaign Act to raise the limits on individual contributions to parties, on party contributions to candidates, and on party spending in publicly funded presidential campaigns.* A minority of us would go even further and double the $25,000 ceiling on an individual's annual political contributions, so that individuals may donate a maximum of $25,000 to party committees while at the same time contributing the present statutory maximum of $25,000 to candidates and nonparty committees.

Such legislation would help diminish the controversial influence of PACs in campaign finance. Given a choice, we also believe that many candidates would rather accept money from broadly based political parties than from PACs. Increased receipts, of course, would permit the parties to offer candidates the services and technologies that are standard features of current campaigns. Some of these party activities are already under way—particularly among the Republicans. Parties able to assist candidates in this way might be better able to maintain those candidates' loyalties to party programs once they are in office. Combined with partial public funding, this measure would diversify funding sources and prevent the monopoly of American campaign finance by a small number of donors.

Admittedly, the reforms we recommend are modest. Nevertheless, they are reasonable and realistic proposals for improving both campaign financing and the conduct of campaigns. We are confident that they fall within the regulatory powers of Congress as delineated by the Supreme Court's *Buckley* ruling. We have no illusions that even these changes will be easy to effect. But modest though they are, the protection of the democratic process is always an urgent duty.

COMMENTS AND DISSENTS

Arthur B. Krim*

Although I concur in the five proposals set forth in the Task Force Report, I cannot accept it as speaking for me. I feel much more strongly than the Report indicates about the gravity of the dangers we are addressing, and I believe that the Report's characterization of the recommended reforms as "modest," rather than "drastic," is a straddle that diminishes, perhaps fatally, the attention that the needed reforms must receive if they are to be enacted.

My recommendations, which accept but go beyond the five proposals in the Report, are based on two strongly felt conclusions: The first is that the recent escalations in the cost of campaigning and the influence of money in politics are endangering the viability of our system of government. The second is that the strength of the two-party system, which, with its stress on broad coalition, has given us relative stability since the Civil War, is now at its lowest ebb in our history. The evidence is overwhelming that the rise of PACs since the *Buckley* decision is at the heart of both of these conclusions.

In my view, PACs have been the principal cause of the runaway escalation in the amounts of money spent in politics, of the corresponding escalation in the perceptions of the influence of money in politics, and of the dangerous breakdown of coalition politics, as best represented by our two major political parties.

It is true that money in politics has been a source of serious concern many times before, never more so than after the 1972 election. But it is also true that Congress, after thorough deliberation, enacted comprehensive legislation in 1974 to defuse the evils of money in federal elections by placing ceilings on contributions and expenditures, both direct and independent. If the 1974 statute had been upheld in toto, any recurrence of potentially venal contributions, as in the 1972 campaign, would have been effectively controlled, the escalating trend of campaign expenditures would have been reversed, and a large measure of equal opportunity and candidate dignity and appearance of integrity would have been restored.

Messrs. Rowe and Price concur.

13

Unhappily, this was not to be the case. The *Buckley* decision, while sustaining limits on direct individual contributions, removed all the ceilings on expenditures, including the ceilings on what a candidate could personally spend on his own election. The decision allowed individual contributions to PACs and from PACs to candidates, and no limit was placed on the number of PACs to which an individual could contribute, so long as it was within the $25,000 annual limit. In addition, the decision opened the door to unlimited so-called independent expenditures, over and beyond what the candidate could legally raise from direct individual PAC contributions, even though these independent expenditures were made expressly to elect or defeat a designated candidate. The inevitable result has been the phenomenal growth of PACs.

The fallout has been dramatic. The single most extensive cause of oversized spending to achieve what should be a public service, and not a self-aggrandizing goal, has been the availability of PAC money. The appearance, if not the fact, of the escalation in the corruptive influence of money in our political process has been caused more by the widespread impression that PAC contributions are based on the expectations of quid pro quos than by any other single factor. In my view, the evils of the latent powers of PACs, in causing lack of respect for a system in which votes appear to be purchasable, exceed the corresponding evils of corporate, labor, or individual power of the wealthy that the 1974 legislation was supposed to correct. And the very thrust of PACs is to bypass coalition in favor of special interests. The evidence is overwhelming that the power of PACs, reaching across state and district lines, erodes the very essence of representational government, on which the major-party coalitions have been built. There is now more than ever a sordid image of many of our legislators thinking more of money sources than of their constituents, of legislators lobbying PACs to be elected, and then, expressly or subliminally, factoring this into their voting decisions when, after their election, the PACs lobby them.

What to do? I believe we must speak out strongly on what can and should be done by Congress to reverse these negative trends before they become fatal. I disagree with the cautions expressed in the Report that to underline the evils of PACs is to court the criticism of "sensationalism" or to make PACs the "scapegoats for many of the ills afflicting our politics." I do not believe that *limiting the money influences of PACs in specific campaigns for or against a candidate* is in some convoluted way a taking away of the rights of groups to have their viewpoints heard—in effect, an attack on a "safeguard against tyranny." It would be unfortunate if, despite the intent of the five proposals, the results of the work of this Task Force end up being used—as the benign language of the Report allows—to condone a status quo that is so obviously seriously flawed.

I think that the objective is to come as close to the 1974 statute as possible. We are dealing with matters legislated by Congress after extended debate, not with new and uncharted objectives. In this context, my principal recommendations are made within the constraints of the *Buckley* decision.

The first is that the ceilings on expenditures in all congressional races, including personal expenditures of the candidates themselves, be reinstated as a condition of acceptance of public financing. Whether or not one is in favor of public financing, or dubious about the possibility of Congress taking such a step, the fact remains that this appears to be the only hope of confining the costs of campaigning to rational limits. Congress wanted the ceilings. It may be reluctant to legislate the public financing that the Supreme Court says it must to support the ceilings. It is now up to Congress, in full possession of the compelling evidence, to explain to the country why the ceiling provisions of any public-financing bill should override any impression of self-serving motivations. I believe this Task Force should help Congress convey that message.

My second principal recommendation is to limit the so-called independent expenditures of PACs. I recognize that the recent opinion of the Federal District Court in Pennsylvania, in declaring a $1,000 limit on such expenditures unconstitutional, casts doubts on hopes of achieving this objective. But neither Congress, by enlarging the limit to more reasonable levels and more carefully defining the point at which "independence" is illusory, nor the Supreme Court, has yet had the final word. There is considerable language in the *Buckley* opinion to justify congressional limitations on such expenditures without infringement of constitutional rights. The basis for this conclusion is the acknowledged power of Congress to regulate PACs and the obvious strength of the argument that allowing unlimited PAC independent expenditures to help elect or defeat a candidate undermines the norms of fairness, equality, and avoidance of corruption accepted by the Supreme Court as proper objectives. As for the First and Fifth amendments, so long as limitations on *true independent expenditures by individuals* are left untouched, there is much language in the *Buckley* opinion to indicate that any particular association mandated by Congress—such as a PAC—that is seeking the same unlimited ceiling could be subject to more restrictive measures. I cite but one of many quotations from the majority opinion in *Buckley* as illustrative:

> Yet, it is clear that neither the right to associate nor the right to participate in political activities is absolute. . . . "significant interference" with protected

rights of political association may be sustained if the State demonstrates a sufficiently important interest and employs means closely drawn to avoid unnecessary abridgement of associational freedoms.

Accordingly, my specific recommendations, which incorporate the thrust of the five proposals contained in the Task Force Report, but go beyond them, are as follows:

1. I favor some system of matching public financing that would incorporate compulsory ceilings for all congressional races. The ceilings would be based on an updating of those contained in the 1974 statute. Provisions should be included so that, if a candidate chooses to reject public funds, the equivalent otherwise available to him will be added—as an automatic increase in ceilings and public contributions—to the funds of any other qualified candidate or candidates.

2. I favor unlimited contributions by individuals to a national party, the state affiliates, or the congressional committees, within the federal ceiling of $25,000 per annum, and unlimited contributions by a national party, the state affiliates, and the congressional committees to candidates, within the mandated ceilings.

3. I favor lower limits on direct expenditures by PACs:

a. a $1,000 limit on contributions to candidates during the primary and general election campaigns (the same as the limit on individual contributions);

b. a statutory limit on the total any candidate can receive from PACs (in the range of $35,000 to $90,000, depending on the ceiling in the particular race);

c. unlimited contributions to a national party, the state affiliates of a national party, and the congressional committees validated by a national party.

4. I favor a $1,000 limit on individual contributions to a PAC and a $5,000 limit on individual contributions to all PACs—all to come within the federal ceiling on individual contributions of $25,000 per annum.

5. I favor stricter governance requirements for PACs, including full disclosure in all solicitations of purposes (direct or indirect), decision-making machinery, eligibility, etc.

6. I favor the strictest possible regulation of independent expenditures by PACs. I strongly urge that:

a. PACs' independent expenditures be subject to a statutory ceiling;

b. more stringent proof of independence be required; a broad definition of collusion or cooperation be established; and strict penalties for violation be enforced;

c. all media copy should include specific attribution, with brief designation of decision-making machinery, percentage of out-of-district contributions, and eligibility for membership;

d. a fair-practices procedure be established to mandate equal time for reply, which should be paid for by offending PACs or made available on a gratis basis by the carrying media;

e. the attacked candidate should have the right to reply without its counting against any compulsory ceiling.

7. While, because of the *Buckley* decision, an individual must be permitted to spend unlimited sums on independent expenditures, I strongly favor requiring full identifying attribution and imposing criminal penalties for any false claim of independence.

Charls E. Walker*

I wish to register my dissent both from some of the underlying assumptions on public financing and on limits on candidate receipts from PACs.

Basic Premises

With all respect for my colleagues in the majority, I do not perceive the status quo in campaign finance as they do. In particular, I do not see strong evidence of a problem or problems that cry out for the fundamental changes in campaign finance that they propose.

On the contrary, I think that there are many signs of health in today's funding of congressional campaigns and many ways in which it

---

Messrs. Gray and Thaxton concur.

is vastly superior to campaign finance before the legislation of the 1970s. Giving and spending is now conducted openly and through legal channels; it is above board and fully reported, with none of the covert and illegal activity of earlier years. Disclosure is now full and complete, and abundant data about campaign finance are now more readily and accurately available than ever before. Millions of Americans are now involved in the campaigns through political contributions to candidates, parties, and PACs, and it is no exaggeration to say that there is now a financial channel or opportunity for virtually every political enthusiasm. In short, we can take pride in our having developed the most open, most broadly based system of voluntary campaign finance in the history of democratic politics. Nor do I think the nation should lightly jeopardize those gains.

The majority's chief argument for change rests on its conclusions about the influence, or perhaps more accurately the perception of influence, of PAC contributions on subsequent votes in Congress. Again, I differ with those conclusions. I do not think that the members of Congress defer so readily in their votes to the wishes of financial contributors, whether these contributors be PACs, parties, or individuals. Like all other contributors and activists, PACs support like-minded candidates, and through their financial support PACs generally seek and gain the same goals that other supporters of successful candidates do. Furthermore, there are very real limits to PAC influence in Congress. Members are pressured from all sides—by party, by lobbyists, by constituents, by presidents, by their own commitments and values, and by all of the workers and contributors in their campaigns. Moreover, the growing diversity of PACs limits the influence of any one of them. When members of the House of Representatives receive an average of $620 from more than one hundred PACs, as they did in 1980, two conclusions are inevitable: The interests of some contributors will certainly oppose those of others, and most congressmen will not be politically dependent on any one PAC or even a small number of PACs.

If there is any lesson to be learned from campaign finance legislation over the past twelve years, it is that forecasts of the consequences have been less than successful. Nothing better illustrates this conclusion than the rise in importance of PACs. The American system of campaign finance is complex and understood only imperfectly. One basic fact should have been learned, though: cash is a very mobile, fluid resource, and if you stop one of its channels, it will flow into others. The problem is that we are not very good at predicting the scale or direction of those new currents. Moreover, legislation must anticipate the consequences of new technological advances in campaigning— cable television or home computers and communication systems, for example—about which we know even less. In short, for the above reasons, there is too great a possibility that major alterations in American campaign finance will create more problems than they will solve.

I do not, however, wish to seem complacent about today's campaign finance. I have joined in several of the recommendations for change expressed in the Task Force Report. I would certainly not rule out change in the future should a need for it be demonstrated. I do remain convinced, however, that the majority has exaggerated the problem and ignored the risks in trying to remedy it. I now turn to their proposed remedies.

Public Finance

I oppose public financing of congressional elections for a wide range of reasons. In contrast to public funding for presidential campaigns, in which there is only one constituency, public funding for congressional campaigns would have to encompass 435 election districts for the House and 50 for the Senate. If a single level of campaign funding (and a single expenditure limit) were designated for all House districts, this would ignore significant differences among them—different areas, different urban-rural mixes, different styles of politics and campaigning, different two-party competitiveness, and different mass-media markets—and thus result in inequities. If a public-funding plan takes into consideration only population differences, similar inequities will occur.

Furthermore, I think that public funding for congressional races will inevitably encounter administrative problems. The cost of compliance will be high for all participants, and the task of the Federal Election Commission will be staggering. I doubt that the FEC will be given the resources or the capacity to meet the challenges of rulemaking, enforcement, reporting, and auditing that will be thrust upon it. A surge of litigation and adjudication will be likely, perhaps resulting in a rise in legally contested elections.

The ultimate political consequences, in my judgment, will be unfortunate. Lower levels of spending will narrow the campaign debate and limit the ability of candidates to communicate with the voters. The funding base for many campaigns may also be narrowed, money may be diverted into independent expenditures, and the competitiveness in congressional elections may be reduced by denying challengers the funds necessary to overcome the advantages of incumbency.

I am concerned about popular reaction to the enactment of a public-funding program. If public opinion polls are to be believed, it will be an unpopular program—one seen by many citizens to be a self-serving attempt by Congress to avoid the tasks of fundraising. Arguments over the administration of a public-funding program may well result in even greater public cynicism about campaign finance.

Limits on Receipts from PACs

The majority of the Task Force supports a new limitation on the freedom of PACs: a limit on the total amount of contributions from PACs that a candidate may accept in an election cycle. (The figure cited in various congressional proposals made in 1983 is in the range of $75,000 to $90,000.) I also dissent from that recommendation.

In considerable part, I oppose such a proposal for many of the same reasons that I oppose the spending limits associated with public financing: the advantage that limiting receipts gives to incumbents, the reduction of campaigning that follows any reduction of receipts or expenditures, and the diversion of PAC funds from contributions to independent expenditures that would result. Furthermore, any reduction in PAC contributions will give one more advantage to candidates able to finance their campaigns out of their own (or their family's) personal fortune.

Finally, such a limit will, I think, have an unequal impact on different kinds of PACs. The effect will probably be the greatest on the larger PACs—especially on PACs making their contributions in large sums. If this should be the case—and I should note that I do not think anyone can confidently predict the result—the limit would impact heavily on organized labor, where a relatively small number of PACs (reflecting the centralization of the labor movement) raise and spend relatively large sums.

Rather than place limits on the acceptance of PAC contributions, I would prefer to promote healthy competition and pluralism in campaign finance. I have, therefore, joined in the unanimous recommendations about strengthening political parties.

Conclusions

I believe that a system of campaign finance ought to meet the following criteria: It should be open and well publicized. It should prevent the monopoly of resources by any one kind or small number of donors. It should provide adequate alternatives to personal wealth as a campaign resource. It should sustain the competitiveness of our politics. And it should finance an ample dialogue in the campaign.

I think today's campaign finance meets those tests surprisingly well. I see no compelling reasons to put it at risk with fundamental changes, the probable results of which we can only dimly perceive.

Herbert Alexander*

Limits on PAC Contributions

The proposal to limit the aggregate amount candidates may accept from PACs would cause more problems than it would solve. In the face of rising campaign costs, the proposal, if enacted, would be counterproductive. Reducing funding from PACs would make it more difficult for many candidates to clarify issues in campaigns and to make their positions known to voters.

A reduction of funding would also benefit incumbents, who begin reelection campaigns with notable advantages: the ability to command greater media attention than most challengers, and allowances for salary, staff, travel, office, and communications whose worth over a two-year term has been estimated at more than $1 million. Further, respected research has concluded that increases in campaign funds generally help challengers more than incumbents and thus lead to more electoral competition. The incremental value of each additional dollar raised and spent by a challenger, in terms of name recognition and possible votes, is much greater than that for an incumbent. To limit PAC giving would make it more difficult for challengers to mount effective campaigns and would increase the power of incumbency.

Reducing the amounts PACs may contribute to candidates, or the amounts candidates may accept from PACs in the aggregate, probably would not reduce PACs' influence on the campaign process; it would merely cause PACs to intensify their efforts to make the voices of their members and sponsors heard through direct and indirect lobbying. Such a legislative change would result in greater diffusion of accountability in the electoral process and would encourage coordination of giving among like-minded PACs.

If reduced direct contributions by PACs to candidates led to an increase in independent spending, then there would be a corresponding loss of control of spending by candidates' campaigns and of accountability to the electorate for political uses of money.

The impact of contribution limitations would be greater on some groups than on others, causing more disparity and imbalance than now exist between business and labor PACs, and between conservative and liberal PACs. For example, the proposal to reduce the amount individual PACs may contribute to candidates would restrict a number of

---

*Mr. Gray concurs on limiting PAC contributions and on strengthening political parties.

large union and membership/health PACs, which give the maximum amount to a relatively large number of candidates, but would have little effect on most corporate PACs, since few of them approach the current $5,000 limit. The proposal to restrict the aggregate amount candidates may accept from PACs, on the other hand, would make it more difficult for candidates who have already accepted the total permitted to campaign effectively in the final days of a highly competitive contest.

Candidates running against opponents who are willing to spend personal funds in their campaigns are at a severe disadvantage. Restrictions imposed on the aggregate contributions that candidates can accept from PACs would further disadvantage candidates without personal means, and would thus threaten the democratic principle of equality of opportunity for qualified persons to seek public office.

Introducing aggregate limits raises constitutional questions of a different order than those raised by either contribution or expenditure limits, on which topics the Supreme Court has spoken. The proposed limits are, in effect, aggregate receipt limits, and candidates would need to pick and choose among proffered contributions to stay under the ceiling. Those who could not contribute because the candidate's limit had been reached could argue that their constitutional right to give was denied, presuming the candidate would have been willing to accept the money had there not been an imposed limit.

There are better ways to offset the development of PACs without unduly restricting their growth or limiting their contributions. One is to raise the $1,000 individual contribution limit, which now is too low. When compared with the buying power of a $1,000 contribution when the limit went into effect in 1975, a $1,000 contribution to a federal candidate is currently worth only about $530.

I believe that the limit on an individual's contributions should be raised to $5,000, and that the overall annual contribution limit, as noted earlier, should also be raised. These actions would make needed funding available to underfinanced campaigns and at the same time would respect the values of diversity and participation in our political system. Further, these actions would increase the individual contribution component of total political receipts and correspondingly decrease the PAC component.

Another means of offsetting PACs, while still allowing for their important contributions to the political system, would be to strengthen the role of the political parties.

Public Funding

For critics of high campaign costs, one of the great attractions of public funding is that it provides the only constitutionally acceptable way to impose campaign expenditure limitations under the Supreme Court's 1976 *Buckley* ruling. The assumption that high campaign costs are universally bad is not well founded, because there are many cases in which high spending is warranted. Regardless of the merits of the arguments, pro and con, on escalating campaign costs, expenditure limits clearly pose problems of their own—particularly in determining a ceiling that is equitable to incumbents and challengers alike. If the ceiling is high, candidates try to spend up to the limit. If it is low, challengers, who may need to spend more money to become well enough known to compete effectively, tend to be hurt. Further, some candidates need to spend more money to raise money than others. In general, spending limits favor candidates who are better known and who have the backing of a superior party organization, celebrity status, or the ability to enlist volunteers. Spending limits tend to reduce the candidate's flexibility when faced with new events or new charges and to diminish the possibility of spontaneity in campaigns—both of which are qualities that help keep the political system vital and healthy.

In addition, expenditure limits tend to trigger independent expenditures, and thus to diminish accountability for the uses of campaign money. The tightly drawn system of expenditure limitations did not work well in the 1980 presidential election. The significant use of independent expenditures—although focused on only a few candidates—pointed up the many opportunities for disbursement on behalf of, or against, a candidate in the pluralistic American system. The concept of expenditure limits, in which the candidate's organization controls spending, is unrealistic when unlimited but coordinated activities by interest groups and party committees are legally sanctioned and unlimited independent expenditures are allowed by court decisions.

The result is two or three simultaneous campaigns—one controlled by the candidate, one coordinated with the candidate, and one entirely outside the candidate's control. The conclusion follows that, if limitations are not effective, they are illusory and breed disrespect for the law; if they are effective, then they tend to inhibit free expression. A false impression of limits serves no purpose; it creates compliance problems and unnecessary bookkeeping costs for the candidates, in that they must keep track of limited expenditures and exempt costs.

Even though the Supreme Court's *Buckley* decision ruled out spending limits without public funding, not all supporters of public funding think that expenditure limits should be bound to public-funding programs. Some supporters advocate public-funding floors rather than spending-limit ceilings. This concept is favored by many mature democracies in Western Europe, where government subsidies are given to political parties with no limits on the receipt or spending of private contributions. The idea is that partial public funding, or a floor, would give candidates in the United States at least minimal access to the electorate and would, by providing alternative funds, allow candidates to reject private contributions that have expressed or tacit obligations attached. By not imposing spending limits, the need to address many of the constitutional issues raised in the *Buckley* case would be avoided. Moreover, caps can be placed on the amounts of public funds disbursed to individual candidates.

Another problem with the Task Force Report recommendation is that it restricts candidates' options. By providing additional public money to those candidates whose opponents choose not to accept public funding, a penalty is imposed for failure to accept public subsidy. No such provision currently exists in regard to the public funding of presidential campaigns, and none is needed. I recommend raising the limit on contributions to a candidate whose opponents choose not to accept public funding, on the theory that those opponents could spend unlimited amounts of money. But raising the limit on contributions does not call for concomitant increases in public funding, as the Task Force Report proposes. In the *Buckley* case, the Supreme Court sanctioned public funding but noted that the option of refusal to accept the money is preserved in the presidential public funding program. The concept of optional public funding is desirable, and penalties should not be imposed for failure to accept the public grant.

Strengthening Political Parties

The Task Force unanimously agreed, for reasons noted in the Report, on the importance of strengthening political parties. I concur with this conclusion and point out the consequent urgency of raising significantly—or abolishing altogether—the present $25,000 overall limit on an individual's contributions in a calendar year. The current limit on an individual's contributions to party committees concerned with election of a federal candidate is $20,000 annually. To urge an increase in the limit an individual can contribute to parties to $25,000, but to retain the $25,000 annual limit on an individual's overall contributions, will not significantly expand donations to the parties and will diminish needed contributions made directly to candidates (as these contributions count against the $25,000 total). As stated, the recommendation will not provide enough additional funding for the parties to enable them to give much more assistance to candidates. Aggregate PAC contributions to Senate candidates in most states where a seat is hotly contested, and to many House candidates, currently exceed both the amounts that party committees can legally contribute to those candidates and the amounts of coordinated expenditures that party committees can spend on their behalf. Many candidates would prefer to receive more money from the parties, and I thus believe that the recommendation should be expanded to permit individuals to contribute larger amounts to the parties. I recommend setting a $25,000 annual limit on an individual's contributions to party committees separate from the current $25,000 annual limit on combined contributions to parties and to candidates for federal office.

The Costs of Establishing and Administering PACs

The Task Force Report did not discuss a significant advantage that those PACs sponsored by corporations, labor organizations, membership organizations, cooperatives, and corporations without capital stock have over those sponsored by issue-oriented and ideological organizations. The law currently permits a corporation or union, for example, to use corporate money or union dues to establish a PAC, to administer a PAC, and to solicit funds on behalf of a PAC. In contrast, issue-oriented or ideological PACs cannot have sponsoring organizations, and hence they must use funds raised under the constraints of contribution limits for the above-mentioned purposes. I recommend that the special exemption for corporations, unions, and other such organizations be repealed so that all PACs will be on an equal footing in terms of raising PAC funds to cover the costs of their establishment, administration, and fund-raising efforts.

Political Action Committees in American Politics: An Overview

A Background Paper
by Frank J. Sorauf

1
INTRODUCTION AND A DEFINITION

In each of the last three federal election campaigns—1978, 1980, and 1982—political action committees (PACs) have shared the mass media with the candidates themselves. Almost every major newspaper and television station has featured an analysis or an explanation of their growth and their importance. Moreover, news reports of candidates' receipts and expenditures focus almost exclusively on PAC money, largely ignoring the individual contributions that still account for well over half of the campaign contributions in federal elections.

It is not hard to understand media and public attention. The sheer growth of national PACs, from 608 in 1974 to 3,371 in 1982, and the lavishness of PAC expenditures—$83.1 million to congressional candidates in the 1982 elections, up from $12.5 million in 1974—are the stuff of which headlines are made.[1] Issues about campaign finance easily translate into more fundamental questions about the distribution of power and influence in American society. And for a media starved for the new and the dramatic, it did no harm that the phenomenon was wrapped in a bold and aggressive rhetoric. The fondness of some committees for the language of violence—"targeting" candidates on "hit lists"—fed the appetite of those straining for simple explanations and devil theories. So much a part of popular political discourse have PACs become that their acronym has come into common usage; millions of Americans know them simply as "packs."

The rapid growth of PAC influence, combined with increases in the money available from all other sources, has in fact set off a broader national concern about the effects of money in American politics. Right or wrong, the belief grows that campaign contributions to candidates lead to influence over their decisions in public office. The belief is all the stronger when PACs that give the money are controlled by organizations that also lobby effectively in legislatures and executive agencies. Concern mounts, too, that the uneven distribution of campaign funds tilts the competitive balance of American politics and makes more probable the victory of incumbents, Republicans, and

29

candidates with personal fortunes. All of those fears lead ultimately to
a conviction that the new availability of political money causes a dis-
ruption in the fundamental distribution of political power in American
society, to new strength for some groups and new vulnerability for
others. Sharp changes in the availability of political resources have
always led to periods of concern and reform, and the decade after 1974
has been no exception.

What, then, are these PACs, which have so clearly become a major
new force in American elections since 1974? They are groups of committees other than party or candidate committees that collect funds
and make expenditures in order to influence the outcome of an election. Most of them—but by no means all—meet additional special
qualifications or characteristics of "multicandidate committees" and
"separate segregated funds." They vary also in the ways in which they
spend to influence elections, most contributing cash, goods, or services
to candidates, but others mobilizing voters or campaigning independently of candidates or parties.

The full significance of the rise of PACs becomes clear only when we
consider their broader role in American politics. Historically, the
major political parties, the Democrats and the Republicans, have been
the organizations that specialized in electoral politics. While they may
have failed at other tasks—organizing legislative majorities, for example—they have dominated the organizing and contesting of our elections. By contrast, interest groups (or, to the less approving, "pressure
groups") have been the organizations that have worked in the policymaking arenas of government. To be sure, parties helped to bring some
measure of discipline to legislatures, and some interest groups
involved themselves in campaigns and elections, but in large measure
the division of labor was observed. Parties were the classic political
organizations for election politics, interest groups for the politics of
policy. The PACs have muddied that neat distinction. They have
many of the organizational instincts and characteristics of interest
groups, and yet they work largely in the electoral province of the political parties.

The phrase "political action committee" does not appear in the statutes of the United States; nonetheless, it is necessary to turn to those
statutes to attempt to understand the phenomenon. Before the 1970s,
the U.S. statutes spoke only of a "political committee," a generic term
that included separate segregated funds (of which, more later), party
committees, and "any committee, club, association, or other group of
persons" that raises and spends more than $1,000 a year.[2] By the time
it wrote the 1974 statutes governing the public financing of presidential elections, Congress had sharpened its definitions. A "political committee" had become:

any committee, association, or organization (whether or not incorporated) which accepts contributions or makes expenditures for the purpose of influencing, or attempting to influence, the nomination or election of one or more individuals to Federal, State, or local elective public office.[3]

It is important to keep in mind that both the statutes and popular usage treat these committees separately from both the committees of political parties and the authorized, official campaign committees of the candidates themselves.

Two other terms in the United States Code complicate this definition of PAC-like committees. First, as a result of the setting of limits on contributions,

The term "multicandidate political committee" means a political committee which has been registered . . . for a period of not less than 6 months, which has received contributions from more than 50 persons, and except for any State political party organization, has made contributions to 5 or more candidates for Federal office.[4]

Most PACs become multicandidate committees because of one powerful incentive. If they qualify as multicandidate committees, they may contribute up to $5,000 to any candidate in any election; if they do not, the limit is $1,000.[5]

The definition of a "separate segregated fund" in federal statutes is accomplished far more obliquely. It emerges from the section of the code that deals with the illegality of contributions made by corporations and labor unions where references are made to "a separate segregated fund . . . utilized for political purposes by a corporation, labor organization, membership organization, cooperative, or corporation without capital stock."[6] Contributions to such separate funds must be voluntary and held apart from the regular treasuries of the founding organizations; their political purposes must also be clearly and publicly stated. Thus PACs of corporations and labor unions must be "separate segregated funds"; those of membership organizations usually are.[7] The separate segregated fund is the instrument by which the funds of a PAC are kept separate from the assets of its parent organization and, as such, is important largely for those PACs whose parent organizations are forbidden to make political contributions directly.

One more clarification in definition is necessary. We tend to think of PACs primarily as very efficient conduits of cash contributions to candidates for public office. Yet some PACs contribute little or no cash to candidates in an election. They, along with any group or individual in American society, may try to influence elections with expenditures independent of either a candidate or a party. The National Conservative PAC, for instance, spent almost all of its $7 million in 1980 in an independent campaign urging the election of Ronald Reagan and the defeat of six Democratic senators. Furthermore, some PACs contribute not cash but services, goods, or expertise to candidates—for example, plane trips, campaign brochures, or courses in campaign tactics. And still other PACs go beyond contributions—in cash or "in kind"— to candidates to engage in other, nonpartisan activities in the campaign. The AFL-CIO Committee on Political Education (COPE), for example, organizes massive voter registration and get-out-the-vote campaigns.

The rise of what appears to be a significant new form of political organization is always important. It is all the more important when the new participants touch the ways in which representative democracy in the United States functions and the ways in which the resources that sustain its competitions are accumulated. Before we examine these issues, however, it is necessary to trace the origins, growth, internal life, and political activities of PACs.[8]

2
THE ORIGINS AND GROWTH OF PACS

Dates of discovery are not necessarily dates of origin. Political action committees may not have dented the consciousness of most Americans until the late 1970s, but they had existed for at least thirty years before then. Although experts disagree about the precise time or place of birth, they do agree that PACs were born within the American labor movement.

In the early years of the twentieth century, Congress prohibited direct contributions to candidates or parties by national banks and corporations. Individual executives, board members, and stockholders were still free to contribute as individuals, though, and there was little in the nature of a regulatory apparatus to stop the unscrupulous few from transferring corporate funds to candidates in some covert way. During World War II, the prohibition against the direct use of funds was extended to labor unions. The Congress of Industrial Organizations (CIO) responded almost immediately in 1943 with what most observers agree was the first PAC: a separate fund set up to receive the voluntary contributions of union members and to spend them in campaigns for public office. On the merger of the American Federation of Labor (AFL) and the CIO in 1955, the resulting AFL-CIO created its Committee on Political Education, the PAC that one scholar has called ". . . the model for virtually all political action committees."[1]

Those PACs whose parent organizations are corporations or trade or membership associations date only from the late 1950s and the early 1960s. Several of the largest of them—the American Medical Political Action Committee (AMPAC) and the Business-Industry Political Action Committee (BIPAC)—were active by the mid-1960s.[2] When Congress wrote the Federal Election Campaign Act (FECA) of 1971, the first comprehensive regulation of campaign finance since the 1920s, labor had almost thirty years of experience with PACs, corporations and associations had much less. The labor PACs were also far more effective than other PACs by any measure of comparison—sums of money contributed, influence exerted, voters mobilized.

The Growth of PACs

The Federal Election Campaign Act and amendments to it in 1974 and 1976 mark the beginning of the modern era for PACs. In fact, the history of PACs in the 1970s is, in one sense, a reflection of legislative and other regulatory developments from 1971 through 1976. Virtually every change in the statutes promoted the growth of PACs, both by directly legitimizing and strengthening them and by limiting the freedom of competing organizations and individuals. That the legislation of the 1970s aided the growth of PACs was scarcely accidental. In 1971, 1974, and 1976,

> organized labor was instrumental in drafting and securing passage of the key provisions relating to PACs in an attempt to improve its own electoral position. . . . The irony of all this is that organized labor unwittingly sowed the seeds that have borne the very fruit it sought to prevent—enhanced business electoral effectiveness—through business use of labor's favorite mechanism, the political action committee.[3]

But, in fairness, labor was not alone in failing to foresee the broad effects of the legislation on the PAC movement; conservatives, too, were confident that Congress had further enhanced the political advantage of labor. It is for good reason that scholars of the legislative process point to the legislation on campaign finance as a major illustration of the "law of unanticipated consequences."

The consequences were not anticipated in large part because the federal regulation of campaign finance is an often uncoordinated amalgam of decisions, made independently in the three branches. And a large number of those separate and uncoordinated decisions created an advantage of one sort or another for the PACs. Consider just these main highlights and their impact on PACs:

• In its massive recodification of campaign finance legislation in 1971, Congress specifically authorized corporations and unions to spend their funds on the establishment and administration of "separate segregated funds." It also regulated some of the activities—especially the solicitations—of the funds. It was the first suggestion of legitimacy for corporate and labor PACs in federal legislation.[4]

• Also in the 1972 legislation, Congress tightened considerably the reporting requirements for all political contributions. The result undoubtedly was to discourage some individual contributions and some practices of dubious legality—and thus to advance the cause of alternatives such as the PACs.[5]

• The 1974 amendments to the FECA—written in the troubled aftermath of the 1972 elections and Watergate—included a limit of $1,000
on individual contributions to a candidate; the limit for a "multicandidate political committee," however, was pegged at $5,000 per candi-
date per election. Moreover, individuals were limited to a total expenditure of $25,000 in an election while no cumulative limit was set for
multicandidate committees. The result obviously was to place greater
constraints on individual contributions than on PACs.[6]

• Also in 1974, Congress removed its prohibition on the formation of
separate segregated funds by contractors with the United States government. Since most large corporations either were contractors with
the national government or would like to be, the removal of the ban
was a spur to the formation of corporate PACs.[7]

• Finally, Congress embarked in 1974 on the greatest innovation in
campaign finance in American history: public funding of the presidential campaign. When both Gerald Ford and Jimmy Carter chose the
public funding option in 1976—and consequently a limit on the contributions they could accept—individuals and groups shifted their
attention to congressional elections, thus stimulating the formation of
multicandidate committees with an interest in congressional politics.[8]

• In 1975, the Federal Election Commission, the regulatory agency
Congress had created to oversee its legislation on campaign finance,
issued its most celebrated advisory opinion. In responding to the Sun
Oil Company's request for advice, it assured Sun that its political
action committee (SunPAC) was a legal separate segregated fund, that
it could contribute to congressional candidates, and that it could solicit
voluntary contributions from all of its employees. For a cautious corporate audience not sure whether the somewhat ambiguous FECA had
actually authorized corporate PACs, there was no longer any doubt.[9]

• In January 1976, in the case of *Buckley v. Valeo,* the Supreme Court
brought the expenditure of money in campaigns under the protection
of the First Amendment. Limiting expenditures on political communication during a campaign, said the Court, necessarily reduces the quan-
tity of expression by restricting the number of issues discussed, the
depth of their exploration, and the size of the audience reached.[10]
    The colloquial observation that "money talks" thus became, for
political purposes, a constitutional principle. More specifically, the
Supreme Court struck down, *inter alia*, the FECA provisions that put
limits on candidates' expenditures and on independent expenditures

made without the knowledge or cooperation of a candidate or party. Thus, the way was opened for candidates to spend increasing amounts of money and for PACs to spend in presidential campaigns even though the candidates had accepted public financing.[11]

There is much more than this to the legislation, advisory opinions, and judicial decisions of the 1970s. Yet the major points are clear. First, a significant number of the major developments in campaign finance laws enacted between 1971 and 1976 opened up opportunities for the growth of PACs. Second, in such a rapid and decentralized explosion of regulation, there was no time or opportunity for testing its consequences, for moving with pragmatic caution, or for weighing the consequences of any one change in the light of others.

So the PACs claimed their birthright in the 1970s and emerged strengthened and enhanced by the new legislation. But that is not to say that they were unscathed; their organization, receipts, and expenditures also came under new scrutiny and new limits.

The new statutory provisions touched the PACs' organizations very lightly. Aside from the requirement that they have a name, a treasurer, and a bank account, their organization and internal processes are their own business. (If a PAC is a separate segregated fund, though, its name must include that of its parent organization. It can no longer masquerade as the "Thrifty Government Political Action Committee.") PACs also must register with the FEC and file periodic reports—as many as seven in an election year—on receipts and expenditures.[12]

The receipts and fund-raising methods of PACs were placed under more comprehensive legislative limits. In any calendar year, a PAC may accept no more than $5,000 from any one contributor and must report to the FEC all contributors of more than $200. However, there are no limits on a PAC's total receipts. Different fund-raising rules apply to different kinds of PACs. Corporate PACs may solicit voluntary contributions from stockholders and executive and administrative personnel (and their families) at their discretion; labor union PACs may do the same from their members. Both corporate and union PACs may solicit each other's main constituency by mail at their homes no more than twice a year. Association PACs also may solicit only members and employees. Moreover, association PACs may solicit the executives and stockholders of corporate members only with the permission of the member corporation, and such corporations may authorize only one solicitation a year. By contrast, unaffiliated PACs (that is, those without parent organizations) are unrestricted in their solicitations.

Finally, the new legislation strictly regulated PAC expenditures. PACs that qualify as multicandidate committees, and most do, may contribute up to $5,000 per election to any candidate for federal office. In a consecutive primary and general election the ceiling thus becomes $10,000. Moreover, a PAC may not give more than $5,000 to any other political committee or more than $15,000 to any party committee in a calendar year. All such limits include both cash and in-kind contributions. Keep in mind that individual contributors are limited to $1,000 per election per candidate and to a total of $25,000 in all federal elections in a calendar year. There is no such aggregate limit for PAC contributions. Like individuals, PACs are not limited in making expenditures that are "independent" of candidates, so long as the expenditures are made without cooperation or consultation with the candidates or their agents.[13]

The Elements of Growth

Whether because of or despite the legislation of the 1970s, the PACs flourished. The deluge of data produced by the legislation's reporting requirements offers all the necessary details and documentation. The major outlines of the growth of PACs are apparent simply by examining the growing numbers of them registered with the FEC (Table 2–1): their numbers more than quintupled in the eight years from 1974 to 1982. While all kinds of PACs proliferated, the major growth clearly took place among the corporate PACs. Just between the presidential election years 1976 and 1980, the number of corporate PACs almost tripled.

Table 2–1 shows the number of PACs registered with the FEC, not the number active in the campaigns of any year. In 1982, only 2,651 of

Table 2-1
Number of PACs Registered with the FEC

Year	Total	Corporate	Labor Union	Association	Unaffiliated	Other
1974	608	89	201	318	*	*
1976	1,146	433	224	489	*	*
1978	1,653	784	217	451	165	36
1980	2,551	1,204	297	574	378	98
1982	3,371	1,467	380	628	746	150

Source: From FEC press releases.

Note: The subcategories are those of the FEC, but I have changed the labels of two of them. What I call "association" PACs, the FEC calls "trade, membership, health" PACs, and what I have called "unaffiliated" PACs (those without parent organizations), the FEC calls "non-connected." The "other" PACs are of two kinds: PACs of cooperatives and those of corporations without stock.

*In the 1974 and 1976 data these categories were apparently lumped with one or more of the three other categories.

the 3,371 registered PACs (79 percent) reported activity; the activity ratio in 1978 was 88 percent and 84 percent in 1980. Thus, while registered PACs increased in number by 104 percent from 1978 to 1982, the number of active PACs grew by 82 percent (from 1,459 to 2,651), still a major increase.[14]

The size of PAC contributions to congressional candidates provides another measure of their impact on American politics. From 1978 to 1982, PAC contributions to candidates for the House and Senate increased by 136 percent (Table 2-2). The growth in contributions made by corporate PACs led the field with an increase of $17.6 million

Table 2-2
**Contributions by PACs to All Candidates for the
House and Senate, 1974-82**
(in millions of dollars)

Year	Total	Corporate	Labor Union	Association	Unaffiliated	Other
1974	12.5	*	6.3	*	0.7	1.0
1976	22.6	*	8.2	*	1.5	2.8
1978	35.2	9.8	10.3	11.3	2.8	1.0
1980	55.2	19.2	13.2	15.9	4.9	2.0
1982	83.1	27.4	20.2	21.7	10.7	3.2

Source: Adapted from Joseph E. Cantor, *Political Action Committees: Their Evolution and Growth and Their Implications for the Political System,* revised edition (Washington, D.C.: CRS of Library of Congress, 1982), p. 87. Data for 1982 from FEC press releases.

Note: For explanation of labels of columns, see Table 2-1.

*No data available for these specific categories in these years.

(180 percent) between 1978 and 1982. While of considerably smaller magnitude, the contributions of the unaffiliated PACs increased at a steeper 282 percent. In comparing these totals across time, however, it is necessary to keep inflation in mind. When the 59 percent rate of inflation between 1976 and 1982 is subtracted from the 268 percent increase in PAC contributions, a real jump of about 200 percent remains.

Perhaps the most revealing measure of the growth of PAC funding is the share of the receipts of congressional candidates that PAC contributions represent. As Table 2-3 indicates, PACs have accounted for a steadily rising share of those receipts and have contributed almost 27 percent of the funds received by all general election candidates for Congress during the 1979-80 election cycle. As the data of Table 2-3 suggest, the funding of congressional campaigns appeared to stabilize in 1982, with the PAC share increasing only slightly and individual contributors still accounting for well over half of the money the candi-

Table 2-3
**Receipts of Candidates in House and Senate General Elections
Contributed by PACs, 1972-82**

Year	House Elections, %	Senate Elections, %
1972	14	12
1974	17	11
1976	23	15
1978	25	13
1980	29	20
1982	31	19

Source: The 1972 to 1978 figures are derived from Michael Malbin, *Parties, Interest Groups, and Campaign Finance Laws* (Washington, D.C.: American Enterprise Institute, 1980), pp. 154-55; 1980 and 1982 percentages computed from data in FEC press releases. The 1982 percentages are calculated using the author's adjustment of preliminary data that the FEC admits are inflated.

dates received.[15] The PACs contributed a higher percentage of the total receipts of House candidates, and a considerably lower percentage for the would-be senators.

While the full and systematic reporting to the FEC enables us to plot the growth of PACs and their activities in federal elections, it is far more difficult to assess their role in the fifty states. State requirements for PAC registration and reporting vary widely, as do the regulatory structures under which PACs operate. Nonetheless, it appears that PACs at the state level are growing just as they are nationally. In Wisconsin, for example, PAC contributions to state and local candidates rose from $362,946 in 1974 to $1,165,273 in 1978—a growth rate of 221 percent in only four years.[16] Between 1976 and 1980, the total number of PACs in California grew by 84 percent, labor PACs by only 5 percent.[17] In the same four years, the number of PACs in Minnesota grew by only 56 percent (probably the result of the state's prohibition against the formation of corporate PACs), but PAC contributions in Minnesota elections increased by 98 percent.[18] The fragments of evidence we have from the states thus are all consistent with the trends at the national level. They also suggest that PACs spend at least as much in state and local elections as they do in campaigns for national offices.

The growth of a "regulatory industry" offers one more bit of testimony to the growth of PACs in the last decade. America's campaigns and elections, like its railroads, have become a regulated activity, and this regulation has spawned lawyers, consultants, accountants, and public relations people specializing in PACs and their relations with the law. A service industry surrounding PACs has also grown up: PAC directories and how-to-start-a-PAC manuals abound, and the entrepreneurs who publish general periodicals and newsletters on political finance have begun to devote increasing attention to PACs.[19] Finally, there are PACs that give advice to smaller, less experienced PACs—PACs' PACs, so to speak.

The Broader Context

Although there is an obvious relationship between the growth of PACs and the development of the regulatory laws on campaign finance, it would be a mistake to see the growth of PACs as simply a result of the new laws. At the most, the regulations of the 1970s created opportunities or options—flashed a green light—for the burgeoning PACs. They created a necessary but certainly not sufficient set of conditions for the PAC explosion. To understand fully the PAC movement, we must look at some fundamental developments in American politics and American society, for the growth of PACs reflects most of the basic changes in American electoral politics since the 1950s. The same factors that contributed to the decline of political parties and party organizations contributed to the growth of PACs and their increasing role in campaigns and elections.

American electoral politics has shifted in the last generation or so to a cash economy. Gone is the barter economy of the political parties that, especially at the state and local levels, historically depended on contributed labor and the in-house expertise of the party functionaries. Candidates did not commission expensive private pollsters to tap local opinion; they relied on door-to-door canvassing by volunteers or party workers. The parties staffed the campaigns of their candidates, asking in return only attention to the interests of the party, especially its patronage interests, should the candidate win office.

In today's politics, however, it is far more common for candidates to organize their own campaigns, assemble their own workers and experts, and raise the considerable amount of cash that these entail. Computer time must be paid for, and mass-media specialists, fund-raisers, and the whole race of campaign managers and consultants work for cash, not for party loyalty, ideology, or patronage. So cash contributors (both individuals and PACs), rather than the parties, now control the essential resources for contesting elections.

At the same time, an educated, informed, and articulate group of largely middle-class citizens over the last generation has been increasing its awareness of things political and the extent of overt participation in politics. In our national obsession with nonvoting—and with hard-core political inactivity and disaffection generally—we often fail to note this increased interest at the other end of the political scale. Some of the activity takes place within the parties, but more of it goes on outside of them—in community politics, in volunteer groups, in individual campaigns, in more traditional interest groups. These educated activists are often motivated by a broad ideology, a cluster of issues, or even a single issue. They reject the relatively issueless politics of traditional party organizations, and they reject, too, the broad, omnibus loyalty to a political party that their parents and grandparents were comfortable with. The new activists want to be selective in their political choices, not to commit their loyalty to a political party and, consequently, to a fully packaged set of candidates and issues.

The purest form of that political selectivity, of course, is the commitment to a single issue and the intense, uncompromising group that espouses it. Single-issue politics produces campaigns, often "negative," to unseat incumbents who have voted "wrong" on one specific issue, regardless of their votes on the many other issues they have confronted. But much of the new selectivity is reflected in commitments to those consistent and related issue positions we call "ideologies." Some of this ideological and issue-centered politics, and its rejection of traditional political compromises and pragmatism, has recently been channeled into the political parties. One need only mention the movements that brought presidential aspirants such as Barry Goldwater, Eugene McCarthy, George McGovern, and Ronald Reagan, as well as the ideologically intense conventions and platform debates of the past two decades. But much of it focuses on interest groups and their PACs, and through them on the candidates and their electoral competition.

Since World War II, there has been an important shift in the basic organization or configuration of American political loyalties. In their heyday, the political parties built their organization on a geographical constituency—on the neighborhood or community that was also the local electoral or representative district. But physical and social mobility began to reorient the American voter.

> Today we are not influenced by neighborhood leaders, but rather by particular occupational and socio-economic group leaders. Consequently our politics are no longer neighborhood based, but directed toward particular occupational or socio-economic groups.[20]

The issue constituency of ideological or interest "proximity" has begun to replace the geographical constituency of physical proximity. There may be a new proximity of the workplace or of occupation, and where there is not, the computer-based mailing list and the United States mails bind those already joined by common concerns. The new technology provides a way to communicate within the new constituency, and the PAC is an efficient and logical avenue for the new political activities.

So, the single issue or the single configuration of issues is replacing in part the broad, all-encompassing political parties, and the new activism is more selective and less partisan. Combined with the decline of the parties' role in campaigns, this new style of politics increasingly produces candidates who, as brokers or political entrepreneurs, organize (with the help of professionals) their own campaigns, assembling the resources and directing their spending. All in all, the new campaign politics fits the PACs like the proverbial glove. Their selective, focused strategies—their desire to achieve limited, specific political objectives—suit today's candidates and today's activists.

It is no exaggeration, therefore, to say that the same factors reducing the role of political parties are also augmenting that of the organized interests, including the PACs. A monumental change is under way in American politics in how we organize political influence. The political parties, which enjoyed their years of greatest influence early in the century, appear to have lost, probably permanently, a good part of their earlier eminence in American politics. PACs, on the other hand, typify the politics of seventy or eighty years later, a politics of greater issue concerns, greater involvement, greater politicization, and greater cash costs.

3
PAC ACTIVITIES AND STRATEGIES

Cash totals are the primary data the PACs report to the Federal Election Commission and thus are the chief measures of their activities in campaigns. Although they do not tell all of the story of the PACs, they tell a great deal. In 1981–82, for example, PACs spent:

• $83.1 million in cash or in-kind contributions to candidates for Congress.

• $4.2 million in contributions to congressional candidates and incumbents not running in 1982. (The major part of that total probably was contributions to help retire campaign debts from earlier election campaigns.)

• $5.3 million in independent expenditures (that is, contributions independent of individual candidates) in the 1982 campaigns, the great majority of which ($3.2 million) was spent by one PAC: the National Conservative Political Action Committee.

• $6.0 million in contributions to political party committees.

Thus PACs spent approximately $98.5 million directly in the national campaigns of 1982. And beyond all of that there are the activities in the elections about which PACs are not required to report: nonpartisan registration and get-out-the-vote campaigns and political exhortations to their contributors.

Such figures, of course, give only the sketchiest outlines of PAC activities in the campaign. Yet from them we can begin to extract the shape of the PACs' role in campaign politics. In looking at the choices they confronted and the decisions they made, we can infer something of their goals, their intentions, and their strategies. Moreover, the patterns of PAC expenditures and contributions permit a more detailed view of the consequences of their campaign activities. The patterns of their spending, in other words, are a mirror of both their internal politics and their external impact.

Direct Contributions to Candidates: Strategic Options

Contributions to candidates remain the chief modus operandi of PACs, accounting for more than $83 million of the $99 million they spent in the 1982 congressional campaigns. They dominate the activities of all kinds of PACs, except the unaffiliated PACs, especially the ideological PACs, which increasingly turn to independent expenditures. (In 1980, the unaffiliated PACs contributed $4.9 million to congressional candidates, but they spent $12 million to $13 million in independent campaigns; even in the absence of a presidential campaign in 1982, they spent $4.5 million independently of the congressional elections.) The overwhelming part of the PACs' direct contributions was made in cash. In the absence of reports on in-kind contributions to the FEC, we must rely on the impressions of knowledgeable observers. Surveys of corporate PACs by the Public Affairs Council, for example, place the percentage making in-kind contributions at well under 5 percent.

Once it has made a general commitment to support candidates with direct cash contributions, virtually every PAC has its own approach to the many sets of strategic options it faces. Since PACs differ enormously in goals, political sophistication, resources, awareness of political possibilities, and the political context in which they function, it is best to be skeptical of generalizations about their activities and operations. Nevertheless, some generalizations are possible. Using the data of the FEC, we can analyze the campaign contributions of PACs from three informative perspectives: incumbents versus challengers, Democrats versus Republicans, and early versus late expenditures. The consequences of the choices among these options are mistakable for American politics, especially if the weight of choice in any one is markedly uneven. Furthermore, those choices offer us the best evidence we have of the intentions and strategies of the PACs in campaign politics. It is what they do, rather than what they say, that most clearly reveals their political purposes.

Although the issues of support for incumbents and of the choice of a party are closely interrelated, they initially deserve separate attention. As Table 3–1 indicates, the PACs have consistently made the great bulk of their contributions to congressional incumbents running for reelection. Giving to incumbents has actually increased in the 1980s. The percentage of funds given to candidates in "open races"—those in which no incumbent is running—diminished significantly, partially

Table 3-1
**PAC Support for Incumbents, Challengers, and Candidates for Open Seats in
Congressional Elections**
1978-82
(percentages)

Year	House			Senate		
	Incumbent	Challenger	Open	Incumbent	Challenger	Open
1978	60.4	18.8	20.8	48.0	29.8	22.2
1980	65.8	20.8	13.4	49.7	38.0	12.3
1982	66.8	17.9	15.3	63.6	23.1	13.2

Source: Reports of the FEC.

because the number of open races dropped from 71 in 1978 to 51 in 1980 and 58 in 1982.

All but one of the different types of PACs fit the general pattern of percentages in Table 3–1. In 1982, for example, corporate PACs, labor PACs, and association PACs all gave between 73.8 and 56.9 percent of their contributions to incumbents. The unconnected or unaffiliated PACs, however, gave the incumbents only 45.6 percent of theirs (in 1980, they gave only 31.5 percent to incumbents). In those differences lie a number of important clues to the nature of PAC activities, and we will return to them shortly.

The FEC's data on the two-party distribution of PAC contributions similarly help one conclude something about the ways in which PACs take party loyalties into consideration in making their contribution decisions. There are substantial differences in the partisan attachments of the various kinds of PACs, as Tables 3–2 and 3–3 make clear. In both 1980 and 1982, labor union PACs gave substantially more than 90 percent of their congressional contributions to Democrats. The contributions of corporate and association PACs are heavily to Republicans, but not so overwhelmingly as the labor contributions to Democrats. The unaffiliated PACs, augmented by such new liberal PACs as Progressive PAC and Democrats for the 80s, are moving collectively to the Democratic party, and the remaining PACs are firmly Democratic, led primarily by the PACs of the cooperatives.

Aside from the turn to the Democrats by the unaffiliated PACs, the division of PAC contributions by candidates of the two parties has been remarkably stable. Still, the 1982 totals reversed a trend that had been running to the Republicans—from 39 percent of PAC contributions in 1976, to 44 percent in 1978, to 47 percent in 1980. Increased labor giving and the turnaround of the unaffiliated PACs in 1982

Table 3-2
**PAC Contributions to Congressional Candidates
by Party, 1980**
(in dollars)

	Democrat		Republican		Other	
Corporate	6,873,811	(35.8%)	12,292,711	(64.1%)	15,600	(0.1%)
Labor	12,360,099	(93.6%)	838,226	(6.3%)	13,400	(0.1%)
Unaffiliated	1,458,694	(29.5%)	3,442,513	(69.6%)	43,451	(0.9%)
Association	6,976,236	(43.9%)	8,871,267	(55.9%)	26,405	(0.2%)
Other[a]	1,226,901	(61.2%)	777,077	(38.8%)	900	([b])
Total	28,895,741	(52.3%)	26,221,794	(47.4%)	99,756	(0.2%)

Source: Reports of the FEC.

a. Includes cooperatives and corporations without stock.

b. Less than 0.1%.

doubtlessly were responsible. Over the last three elections, moreover, the trend appears to support the claim that PACs find it easier to raise money to give to likely winners and that they hesitate to contribute to prospective losers. In all three, PAC dollars moved to the party expected to pick up seats in the congressional elections: the Republicans in 1978 and 1980, and the Democrats in 1982.

These aggregate summaries provided by the FEC do not give us answers to several questions about the party preferences of PACs. We cannot say what proportion of individual PACs give entirely (or largely) to candidates of one party and how many have a more clearly bipartisan strategy. (It is plain, though, that most labor PACs do not employ

Table 3-3
**PAC Contributions to Congressional Candidates
by Party, 1982**
(in dollars)

	Democrat		Republican		Other	
Corporate	9,384,166	(34.3%)	17,987,726	(65.7%)	975	([a])
Labor	19,064,623	(94.6%)	1,091,874	(5.4%)	550	([a])
Unaffiliated	5,442,574	(50.9%)	5,240,837	(49.0%)	12,160	(0.1%)
Association	9,264,333	(42.6%)	12,449,102	(57.3%)	8,500	([a])
Other[b]	1,944,371	(61.4%)	1,222,442	(38.6%)	—	—
Total	45,100,067	(54.3%)	37,991,981	(45.7%)	22,110	([a])

Source: Reports of the FEC.

a. Less than 0.1%.

b. Includes cooperatives and corporations without stock.

a bipartisan stragegy.) Nor can we easily relate liberal-conservative preferences to choices between candidates of the two parties. Is it possible, for example, that corporate PACs are supporting Southern Democrats much more heavily than Democrats from the North? If so, their "bi-partisan" giving might well be more ideologically consistent than it seems at a quick glance.

Table 3–4 suggests some of the complexities of the relationships between partisan giving and giving to incumbents. It is first worth noting that the table clarifies the party-ideological preferences of the different types of PACs through the choices they make when no incumbents are running.[1] Next, it should be kept in mind that, as voters went to the polls in 1982, 58.4 percent of the incumbents running for the House and 63.3 percent of those running for the Senate were Democrats; consequently, almost all of the difference in support for incumbent Democrats and incumbent Republicans can be explained by their different numbers.

However, Table 3–4 is most revealing when the totals for 1982 are compared with those for 1980 (Table 3–5). The Democratic superiority among incumbents was reduced in 1982, as was the Republican superiority among challengers. In part these changes reflect the lower numbers of Democratic incumbents in 1982 (58 and 63 percent, respectively, in the House and the Senate, versus 63 and 71 percent in 1980). In part, too, they reflect a shift from challenger to incumbent support as a matter of conscious strategy by corporation, unaffiliated, and association PACs. All three sharply increased their support for Republican

Table 3-4
PAC Contributions to Incumbent, Challenger,
and Open Seat Candidates for Congress
by Party Affiliations, 1982
(percentage)

	Incumbent		Challenger		Open Seat		Total [a]
	Dem.	Rep.	Dem.	Rep.	Dem.	Rep.	
Corporate	29.9	42.6	1.6	11.7	2.8	11.4	100.0
Labor	52.4	4.5	27.5	0.1	14.7	0.8	100.0
Unaffiliated	26.9	18.7	15.5	19.3	8.5	10.9	99.8
Association	34.2	39.6	4.5	8.6	4.0	9.1	100.0
Other [b]	50.9	30.6	5.4	2.2	5.1	5.9	100.1
Total [c]	36.9	29.0	10.6	8.7	6.8	8.0	100.0

Source: Reports of the FEC.

a. Totals are other than 100 percent for one of two reasons: rounding errors and the exclusion of minor-party candidates.
b. Includes cooperatives and corporations without stock.
c. The total sum here is $83,114,158.

Table 3-5
PAC Contributions to Incumbent, Challenger,
and Open Seat Candidates for Congress
by Party Affiliations, 1980
(percentage)

| | Incumbent | | Challenger | | Open Seat | | Total [a] |
	Dem.	Rep.	Dem.	Rep.	Dem.	Rep.	
Corporate	32.0	24.6	1.6	29.6	2.2	10.2	100.2
Labor	65.5	5.5	16.1	0.5	12.0	0.3	99.9
Unaffiliated	20.8	10.8	4.7	44.2	4.0	14.6	99.1
Association	37.5	26.7	2.8	20.2	3.7	9.0	99.9
Other [b]	54.7	22.6	2.1	8.4	4.4	7.7	99.9
Total [c]	41.4	19.3	5.7	20.4	5.2	7.8	99.8

Source: Reports of the FEC.

a. Totals are other than 100 percent for one of two reasons: rounding errors and the exclusion of minor-party candidates.
b. Includes cooperatives and corporations without stock.
c. The total sum here is $55,217,291.

incumbents while cutting support for Republican challengers drastically. Finally, they mirror also a growing ideological heterogeneity among the association and unaffiliated PACs.

There are two corollaries to the axiom of PAC support for incumbents: the majority factor and the seniority factor. If we assume that PACs support incumbents primarily to gain access to powerful men and women in Congress, we would expect a disproportionate amount of PAC money to go to incumbents of the majority party and to individuals of high seniority in it—that is, to the members of Congress who hold either party leadership positions or committee or subcommittee chairmanships. In 1980, House committee chairs running for election received 44 percent of their campaign funds from PACs. But since all House incumbents received 37.6 percent from PACs, the difference is less than one might expect in view of the power of majority and senior incumbency. (It bears noting, however, that incumbents in leadership positions probably raise more money on the average than ordinary incumbents and that they tend to have safer districts; under those circumstances, the 44 percent figure is perhaps more impressive than it seems at first.) Senate committee chairmen, on the other hand, receive no more PAC money than other senators. That fact may well be a reflection of the lesser power of committees and their chairmen in the Senate.[2]

How can we explain the fondness of PACs for incumbents? Most PACs have parent organizations, and most of those organizations have legislative interests and Washington representatives. They do not want that legislative position compromised, their legislative contacts angered, their representations generally made more difficult. Supporting incumbents is thus a strategy of risk avoidance, of consolidating and protecting influence already won; it is the strategy of the already influential. Furthermore, since incumbents are more likely winners and challengers are more likely to be political long shots, many PACs support incumbents in order to build an acceptable "win-loss" record in the candidates they support. Caution in campaign finance is more than a conviction; it is almost an imperative for the organization with legislative goals, and a shift away from the incumbent strategy is safe for the cautious only when the incumbents stand to lose.[3]

Even so, some PACs with parent organizations follow the more ideological strategy of backing challengers and preferred candidates in open races. How does one explain such an apparent contradiction? There are of course several factors affecting the balance between a pragmatic and ideological legislative strategy, but one appears to stand out: the extent to which PAC giving is integrated into the parent organization's legislative representation. Take the classic case of a corporate PAC run out of the corporation's Washington office. The personnel of that office represent the corporation before Congress and executive agencies and may in fact run the PAC, at least to the extent of making its political decisions. Their inclination is to preserve contacts and to ensure themselves a friendly hearing in Congress. They also are importuned by members of Congress to buy tickets to fundraising dinners, and it is convenient to have PAC funds with which to do so. The PAC officers or participants back at company headquarters, on the other hand, may be far less sympathetic generally with incumbents—more sympathetic, in fact, with the idea of throwing the rascals out—and better acquainted with the challengers in the constituencies. The Washington people tend to favor one strategy; the people at company headquarters tend to favor another. The point at which the compromise is struck between them is often an indication of the strength of the Washington representatives in the PAC decision-making.

In contrast stand the unaffiliated, often ideological PACs, which gave only 46 percent of their 1982 contributions to incumbents. No parent organization's interests hamper or temper their decisions. They are less inclined to be pragmatic, less accepting of the compromises of successful incumbents. Often profoundly committed to change, they are less willing to support the status quo and its agents, less inclined to pursue the "legislative strategy" of keeping doors open in Congress.

The third strategic question facing PACs—and our third perspective for exploring them—concerns the timing of the PAC contribution. While the issue is large and complex, the decision primarily reflects the extent to which the PAC wishes to undertake risks in its campaign strategy. To a very great extent, after all, the early gift is the risky gift, especially if it is given in primary elections. But when the risks are greatest, the stakes and the possible payoff are also the greatest, not only in determining who sits in Congress but also in obtaining the winner's full measure of gratitude. The size of the risk and the magnitude of the potential gain are thus directly related.

Since PACs with parent organizations tend to seek low-risk contribution strategies, we thus might expect their money to be late money. However, Table 3-6 indicates that more than 42 percent of the PAC money in 1980 and nearly 46 percent in 1982 had been given by the

Table 3-6
Timing of PAC Contributions to Congressional Candidates, 1980 and 1982

| | Percentage of Total Contributions Given by: | |
	June 30, 1980	June 30, 1982
Corporate	44.8	51.4
Labor	44.2	43.0
Unaffiliated	27.0	28.5
Association	43.1	49.6
Others	42.0	46.8
Total	42.5	45.7

Source: For the 1980 figures, the FEC Interim Report Number 9 for 1979-80. For 1982 figures, the FEC Interim Report Number 9 for 1981-82.

end of June. While standards of "early" and "late" may differ from state to state because primary elections can be held any time from spring to September, this pattern of distribution is neither clearly early nor egregiously late. Only the unaffiliated PACs lag behind the pace of the other PACs. They would thus appear to combine a "risky" strategy in independent expenditures with considerable risk avoidance in their direct contributions.

The timing of contributions reflects several other considerations, not the least of which is the sheer availability of funds. Money received late must be given late. Some PACs, too, protect their won-lost percentage by making their contributions late in the campaign when the results are at least predictable within certain margins of error. Increasingly, PAC managers and observers of the PACs talk of the importance of "start-up money" or "seed money" for campaigns: the early money that gets the campaign started, establishes its credibility, and enables it to begin the solicitation of additional money. But the very concept of start-up or seed money defines it as money for the challenger or the candidate in an open race. It is, therefore, surprising that the very PACs that contribute the largest percentages to challengers—the unaffiliated ones—are the ones that contribute latest in the campaign. The explanation of the anomaly appears to lie in fundamental political practicalities: unaffiliated PACs cannot raise money, and thus cannot spend it, before the heat and excitement of the campaign. Although PACs as a whole had raised 63 percent of their 1979–80 receipts by June 30, 1980, the unaffiliated PACs had only 44 percent of their total funds by then.[4]

Observers of PACs have hypothesized that, as PACs become older and more mature, they will be more willing to give earlier in the campaigns. It is part of a persuasive "developmental" theory of PACs: that the PACs become more risk-tolerant, more confident, and more sophisticated politically as they mature. FEC data do not directly address the question of timing, but the data in Table 3–6 suggest that PACs are moving to earlier contributions. Whether that changing timetable reflects greater political sophistication, the sheer availability of funds to give, or the earlier development of the candidacies themselves is a trickier question of interpretation.

Apart from these three intertwined questions of strategy about direct contributions, a fourth deserves mention: the issue of cash versus in-kind contributions. Although the FEC has no systematic data on the extent of in-kind contributions, most observers do not think they are extensive. Money is still the currency of campaign politics. But there are exceptions. Alliance for Politics, the PAC of the Chamber of Commerce of the United States, contributes only goods and services to candidates, including:

> a clearinghouse of candidate and election information gleaned from nationwide research; trained people to help organize and instruct campaign leaders and workers in selected races; experts to advise candidates on media relations; and research on issues, voting records, and economic forecasts for specific congressional districts.[5]

Other PACs mix cash and in-kind help. The National Committee for an Effective Congress gives money, but it also offers polls, legal advice, and political information through its Campaign Services Project.

If in-kind contributions have not increased, it has not been for a lack of urging. There are those in the PAC movement who are much put off by the improvisations of most campaigns and who would like to see new organizational skills improve the chances of the candidates they support—to protect their political investments, as it were. Some, too, would relish a more active role in the campaign. But the urge to shift from cash to in-kind contributions—and thus to take a more interventionist role in the campaigns—has faltered, notwithstanding the many kinds of organizational, media, accounting, and personnel expertise many PACs command. Why? Candidate resistance for one thing. Candidates want to run their own campaigns. Having recently escaped party control, they are not anxious to accept fresh campaign bondage. In addition, the political inhibitions of many organizations restrain their own PACs. Corporations and membership associations, especially, are often newcomers to politics, and they are not yet ready for such active roles in campaigns.

As we have the opportunity to analyze more elections, it becomes clear that the search for consistent strategies in the political decisions of PACs is fruitless. They react to the specific events, opportunities, and context of each election campaign. Thus corporate and association PACs, for example, shifted back to greater support for Republican incumbents in 1982 in order to protect earlier gains and in response to an unfavorable prognosis for further gains by Republican challengers. In general, experience in campaign politics and its accompanying political sophistication seem to bring the PACs not to a greater ideological purism but, rather, to a greater political realism and adaptability, and to a greater willingness to pursue the short-run political goal.

Independent Expenditures: New Options

When the Supreme Court, in *Buckley v. Valeo,* protected independent campaign expenditures by striking down a limit on them legislated by Congress in 1974, it established them as a genuine alternative to direct contributions.[6] In the post-*Buckley* amendments of 1976, Congress then defined an independent expenditure as

> an expenditure by a person expressly advocating the election or defeat of a clearly identified candidate which is made without cooperation or consultation with any candidate, or any authorized committee or agent of such candidate, and which is not made in concert with, or at the request or suggestion of, any candidate, or any authorized committee or agent of such candidate.[7]

Thus the right to make independent expenditures in campaigns was brought under the aura of the First Amendment. It was not long before a few PACs responded.

The FEC data on independent expenditures for 1976 are incomplete, but probably all independent spenders—PACs, other groups, and individuals—spent approximately $2 million in that year, $1.6 million in the presidential campaign and the rest in the campaigns for Congress.[8] By 1978, the FEC began to account separately for independent expenditures by PACs, and its data since then document the enormous

Table 3-7
Independent Expenditures by PACs, 1978-82
(millions of dollars)

	1978	1980	1982
Presidential campaign	—	12.0	—
Congressional campaign	0.3	2.2	5.3

Source: Reports of the FEC.

growth in them (Table 3–7). Moreover, the FEC's data also document the relative importance of the PAC in the realm of independent expenditures: in 1980 they accounted for $14.2 million of the total of $16.0 million spent by all groups and individuals.

Independent expenditures by PACs differ from their direct contributions to candidates in a number of important ways. First, in 1980, they came heavily from unaffiliated PACs rather than from the PACs of unions, corporations, or associations. The PACs without parent organizations accounted for $13.1 million of the $14.2 million PAC total. The spending of the unaffiliated PACs was led by Senator Jesse Helms's Congressional Club ($4.6 million) and NCPAC, the National Conservative Political Action Committee ($3.3 million).[9]

Second, PACs could not make direct contributions to presidential candidates in 1976 and 1980 because the candidates chose public financing with its attendant limits on contributions and expenditures. So, although they were free to make contributions in the prenomination phase of presidential politics (but few did), independent expenditures were the only avenues of influence open to them in the election campaign. Only a small number of PACs entered it, but they did so in an impressive way in 1980. The Congressional Club—its name notwithstanding—spent $4.6 million on behalf of Ronald Reagan's candidacy, and NCPAC added another $1.9 million in support of Reagan. Moreover, two new ad hoc unaffiliated PACs, Americans for Change and Americans for an Effective Presidency, together spent almost $2 million in support of the Reagan candidacy while making no other political expenditures in 1980.

Third, independent expenditures lend themselves uniquely to "negative" campaigning. In 1980, NCPAC brought that strategy to national attention by spending more than $1.2 million to oppose the reelection of six liberal Democratic senators. (Of the six, four lost: Birch Bayh of Indiana, Frank Church of Idaho, John C. Culver of Iowa, and George McGovern of South Dakota; Thomas Eagleton of Missouri and Alan Cranston of California won.) Of the $5.3 million that PACs spent independently on the congressional elections of 1982, 77 percent was spent in opposition to (rather than in support of) a candidate. Such negative expenditures are especially suited to the campaigns to unseat incumbents; they are easily focused on the voting record and political reputation of the incumbent, and they can adopt a harder edge than the challenger might be comfortable with in his own campaign.

Fourth, the independent campaigns are by definition outside of the control of candidates and parties. They may in fact be carried on despite the active displeasure of the party or candidates ostensibly benefiting from them. Voters may vote against a candidate whose campaign tactics they disapprove of, but they hold no sanctions against a group waging a distasteful or unethical campaign independent of either candidate.

Fifth, while direct contributions by PACs to congressional candidates are fairly closely divided along party lines, Republicans have an overwhelming advantage in their independent expenditures. In 1980, $13.8 million of the total of $14.2 million in PAC independent expenditures, or a shade over 97 percent, was spent in support of Republicans or in opposition to Democratic candidates. In the 1982 congressional elections, the comparable figure was approximately 85 percent.

Finally, much of the reputed power and effectiveness of the independent campaigns comes from their experienced use of the mass media. They are creatures of modern technology, their funds raised with the help of high-speed computers and spent on electronic media.[10]

Independent spending by PACs grew for different reasons in the presidential and congressional campaigns. In the presidential election of 1980, PACs, especially the ad hoc PACs, served as vehicles for money that could not be given directly to candidates who had agreed to accept public financing instead of direct contributions. The growth of spending in congressional elections is largely the doing of one PAC: NCPAC by itself accounted for 60 percent of the $5.3 million PACs spent independently in 1982. That involvement reflects the aggressive politics, negative campaigning, and militant conservatism that NCPAC and its executive director, Terry Dolan, have fashioned into a special political style. Beyond the NCPAC phenomenon, a few large corporate and association PACs also increased their independent spending in 1982, largely as a way of adding to their direct support of candidates. If those PACs continue to increase their receipts and if contribution limits remain fixed, they may well further increase their independent spending.

The future of independent expenditures in the 1984 presidential campaign is especially uncertain in view of the FEC's intention to enforce limits on them. In its 1976 *Buckley* decision, the Supreme Court never addressed the constitutionality of the limit of $1,000 on independent expenditures in support of a presidential candidate taking public funds (and the spending limits that accompany them). When the issue went to a federal district court in 1980, a three-judge panel, following the logic of the *Buckley* decision, declared the section unconstitutional. In 1982, the Supreme Court, without opinion, upheld the decision of the district court on a 4–4 division. (Justice Sandra Day O'Connor did not take part in consideration of the case.)[11] However, in May 1983, the FEC announced that it did not consider this outcome to have settled the constitutional issue and that it would enforce the $1,000 limit in 1984. By the summer of 1983, interested parties were again rushing to the federal courts for another test of the provision and the FEC's course of action.[12]

4
LINKAGES BEYOND THE PAC

Political parties, interest groups, and now political action committees demonstrate the truth of the axiom that the political influence of individuals linked together in organizations is greater than the sum of their influence as individuals. Organization in itself is thus a major source of political influence and of the suspicion and regulation it engenders.

PACs per se achieve only a first level of organization or aggregation. They bring together individual contributors for a limited task and for appropriate limited goals. But the process of building aggregates of influence or activity need not stop at that point, and many of the watchdogs of PACs fear it has not. Additional linkage may be of two kinds. The first is simply the organization of individual PACs into coalitions or alliances of PACs. As the number of PACs in national politics climbs above 3,000, individual PACs may well feel the need for friends, allies, and mentors. The second form of possible linkage is more complex. It involves the capacity of a PAC to link its activities in electoral politics to activities elsewhere in the political process—especially in registering and turning out voters and in lobbying in American legislatures.

Cooperation Among PACs

The most conspicuous record of cooperation and joint activity among the PACs, that of the unaffiliated conservative PACs of the new right, is the most conspicuous simply because it is the most widely reported, the result of a massive case of journalistic curiosity in and after the 1980 elections. Among the PACs of the right, there is sharing of information, joint interviewing of candidates, overlapping leadership, and some cooperation in strategy and tactics. Senator Jesse Helms founded his own Congressional Club, helped found the Conservative Caucus, and serves as honorary chairman of the Coalition for Freedom.[1] Much of the cooperation among the PACs of the right pivots about Richard Viguerie's direct mail lists and facilities that serve, among others,

NCPAC, the Conservative Caucus, the Congressional Club, and the
Committee for the Survival of a Free Congress. Moreover, NCPAC
and Helms's Congressional Club worked closely in their campaigns of
independent expenditures in the 1980 elections. According to Terry
Dolan of NCPAC, they planned cooperatively on "concepts and ads"
in support of Ronald Reagan.[2]

Beyond the sketchy look into the network of conservative organizations and PACs, we can only speculate. Certainly other PACs do coop-
erate, work out informal divisions of labor, and develop complemen-
tary strategies. Notes *Business Week* about corporate PACs:

> Just as important in helping increasingly sophisticated PACs choose their
> candidates . . . are informal contacts among PAC administrators, who
> often are their companies' government relations or corporate communica-
> tions vice-presidents. The seminars and meetings they attend around the
> nation have led to the formation of a new kind of intelligence network that,
> in many cases, helps PAC members evaluate candidates. "There is a net-
> work," says ARCO's [Robert] McElroy. "I provided information to another
> PAC on a local race recently. Four years ago that wasn't possible."[3]

In addition, many corporate or labor PACs work out informal divisions of labor to make their resources go as far as possible on behalf of
similar interests. The joint interviewing of candidates, for instance,
leads to some of that cooperation.

But by far the greatest amount of cooperation among PACs results
not from alliances but from a hierarchy of function or expertise. More
than 3,000 PACs have money, but a far smaller number command the
information, judgment, and political skills with which to operate effectively. Within the various kinds of PACs, therefore, networks develop
around those PACs with the critical expertise. The *New York Times*
provided an example midway in the 1982 campaign:

> Mr. Kochevar is the director of the political arm of the Chamber of Com-
> merce, and next week he will be introducing a new wrinkle into the complex
> and competitive world of political fundraising. Using satellite linkups, the
> Chamber will present a closed-circuit television show for about 250 man-
> agers of . . . PACs, gathered in seven cities around the country.
>
> The purpose of the five-hour session is to convince the managers to con-
> tribute money to the Congressional candidates, about 100 or so, favored by
> the Chamber. The pitch will include videotaped appeals by many of the
> hopefuls, plus a sampling of their television commercials.[4]

The AFL-CIO's Committee on Political Education (COPE) has classi-
cally played this kind of leadership role within the labor movement, as
has the Business-Industry PAC (BIPAC) among the business PACs.

But more than expertise moves in these networks; so does cash.

Some PACs receive and spend money contributed by other PACs. In 1980, a total of $1,768,836 was transferred from one PAC to another. The largest recipients, and thus the most significant of these financial brokers, were the COPE of the AFL-CIO ($349,329), the PAC of the International Brotherhood of Electrical Workers ($121,740), the American Bankers Association PAC ($108,831), BIPAC ($88,018), and the United States League of Savings Associations PAC ($74,561).[5]

There are, though, at least two limits to such cooperation among PACs. One is the divergence of interests among them. The interests of craft and industrial unions diverge, and so do those of conservationist PACs and PACs in the energy industries, those of the coal and the oil industries, even those of oil corporations with large foreign holdings and those without them. The second constraint is legal. Federal law requires PACs to maintain their operating independence; otherwise they run the danger of being found "affiliated" and thus subject to the contribution limits of a single PAC.

Relationships between PACs and the major parties are more obscure, but at the national level at least the cooperation and interaction are readily apparent. By the late 1970s, the national committees of both parties had begun to solicit PAC contributions. They and the parties' congressional campaign committees steer needy candidates to the appropriate PACs. In 1979, the PAC liaison specialist for the Republican National Committee—a revealing title in itself—observed to a journalist:

We give a challenger or open-seat prospect a list of every PAC that exists. From there, we try to determine which committees will have a philosophical affinity for the candidate and find out whether the PAC has an interest in the candidate's district.[6]

Sometimes the auspices are less official. An enterprising local public relations man organized a forum for 30 congressional candidates and 130 PAC representatives at the Republican national convention in Detroit in the summer of 1980.[7]

Even though the parties and the PACs are in a general sense competitors for the loyalties of candidates, their sharing of the resources and symbols of campaigning force them inevitably into loose alliances. They are, however, more alliances of recognition than of active cooperation.

The Legislative Connection

Beyond mere alliances, PACs achieve linkages in function. The classic, even quintessential link is that between their contributions in campaigns and the congressional lobbying activities of their related organizations. It is a joining of influence in one part of the political process to influence in another part, with a consequent multiplication of the magnitude of influence. It is this very network or concatenation of influence that most concerns many of the would-be reformers of the PACs. To put the point rather simply, groups such as Common Cause and Congress Watch fear the ability of the PACs to join legislative and electoral politics more efficiently and purposefully than they have been joined in the past. Writes Fred Wertheimer of Common Cause:

> There is a *qualitative* difference in our political system between individual contributions which may or may not be tied to organized lobbying efforts and money from PACs—which almost always is.[8]

It is a concern given substance by the pattern of contributing heavily to powerful incumbents and focusing contributions on members of committees handling specific areas of legislation. In the words of the preface to a Common Cause report:

> Although explicit *quid pro quos* are rarely involved, PAC dollars often provide the donating groups with a degree of access and influence with Members [of Congress] unavailable to the average constituent.[9]

Two themes thus recur: the greater purposefulness of organizations, and the inequality of political resources and influence.

It is not difficult to establish a connection between electoral contributions and legislative lobbying. Several studies demonstrate that at least some PACs funnel their contributions to members of the committee in Congress that acts in the policy areas in which they are interested. It is also undeniable that those PACs—or more precisely, their parent organizations—often lobby for their legislative goals in those committees.

Much of this line of argument is anecdotal; that is, it rests on a small number of vivid examples of PAC-interest group successes. The most widely publicized of them recently involved the attempts of the Federal Trade Commission (FTC) in mid-1982 to propound a regulation requiring used-car dealers to disclose a car's known defects on a window sticker. The regulation was subject to legislative veto, and both houses of Congress voted to overturn it by majorities in excess of 2–1.

All of that would have appeared as little more than a congressional reining in of the FTC had it not been for the campaign finance activities of the PAC of the National Automobile Dealers Association (NADA). It had contributed more than $1 million to federal candidates in the 1979–80 election cycle, and its contributions for 1981–82 were substantially larger. (In 1979–80, it was the third-largest contributor among all of the association PACs.) One newspaper account reported that it gave more than $800,000 to more than 300 members of Congress over the three years from 1979 to 1982. The same source estimated that "about 85 percent" of the recipients voted against the proposed FTC rule and that some months earlier sixteen of them had agreed to cosponsor the resolution of disapproval shortly after receiving campaign contributions from the NADAPAC.[10]

It is not clear, however, how representative such relationships between campaign money and legislative votes are of all of the votes and PAC activity in congressional politics. We do not keep a count of instances in which PACs fail to achieve their legislative goals. Nor do we know what percentage of PACs pursue such specific legislative objectives rather than the more general goals of electing congenial and supportive legislators. Moreover, we have no technique or method of separating the effect of the campaign contribution from the effect of the more conventional lobbying. The car dealers, drawing on a membership of 20,000 spread all across the country, were obviously not without political influence even without making campaign contributions.

We are still uncertain, therefore, about the extent of the coordination or integration of PAC campaign finance and organizational lobbying. Many organizations pursue a general political strategy in PAC campaign contributions and a more immediate, targeted activity in their lobbying. Yet while the linked activities are separate and perhaps not fully coordinated, they are surely not uncoordinated either. Both serve the same basic interests of the parent organization. And, most important, organizational lobbying accounts for the most common extension of PAC influence beyond electoral politics. Labor, corporate, and association PACs do not ignore the legislative goals of their parent organizations.

Mobilizing the Voters

The linkage between campaign contributions and lobbying is a linkage forward in time, focusing first on the election of candidates and then on their subsequent policymaking. The other functional linkage the PACs achieve remains within the time span of the campaign but links electoral politics to voter mobilization. In fact, the federal statutes on campaign finance recognize and protect such mobilizations by excluding them from spending limits. For the purpose of reporting and disclosure to the FEC, therefore, the term "expenditure" does *not* include:

> nonpartisan activity designed to encourage individuals to vote or to register to vote.

Or,

> any communication by any membership organization or corporation to its members, stockholders, or executive or administrative personnel . . . expressly advocating the election or defeat of a clearly identified candidate. . . .[11]

In the latter instance, however, if the cost of the communication exceeds $2,000 for any election, it must be reported to the FEC.

Historically, organized labor has most extensively undertaken these communication activities. In 1980, for example, labor groups incurred 75 percent of the "communication costs" (roughly $3 million of $4 million) reported to the FEC. They have very large numbers of loyal members, already organized and mobilized for economic goals, a significant portion of whom would probably not register or vote without mobilization. These points are important because Republicans and conservatives take note of them when arguing that the electoral influence of labor unions must be measured not only by their direct contributions to candidates but also by their ability to register, prompt, and turn out a vote for Democratic candidates.

American corporations, on the other hand, do not have the political tradition that labor has. They do not have the mechanism for endorsing candidates and bestowing legitimacy on endorsements that labor does. Nor do corporations have the necessary internal support for political action, either from their employees or their stockholders. Fear of stockholder suits in the event of the political use of corporate funds may be a considerable deterrent to a broader political role for them. Therefore, corporations and their PACs find it easier to mobilize money then people.

A closer look at all of the 1980 communication costs details the labor stake more fully. A total of $3,971,559 in such costs was reported to the FEC by a total of sixty-two organizations. (In 1976, seventy-one organizations spent $2.1 million; labor accounted for 94 percent.)

• Fifty-seven of the sixty-two organizations were labor organizations (four were associations and one was a corporation).

• Seventy-five percent was spent by labor.

• Communications on behalf of or opposed to Jimmy Carter's candidacy for the presidency accounted for $1.6 million (41 percent) of the total.

• Virtually all of the nonlabor expenditures, $803,839, were spent by one organization, the National Rifle Association.

But these totals underestimate actual endorsements. Groups and organizations must report only communications about specific candidates; advice to "vote Democratic" or "vote Republican" need not be reported. Nor do groups have to report communications about candidates in publications—such as regular union periodicals—whose main content is not political. Nor do they have to report communication costs of less than $2,000.

The registration and get-out-the-vote expenditures are much more difficult to estimate because federal statutes do not require that they be reported. Both corporations and unions engage in them, but the magnitude of labor programs is undoubtedly far greater. Legally and formally, of course, they are nonpartisan activities, but labor proceeds with them on the assumption that most of the voters it sends to the polls will support candidates endorsed by organized labor. And with the stakes as large as the activation of millions of voters, the expense is not inconsiderable. Michael Malbin, a resident fellow at the American Enterprise Institute, estimated that in 1976 registration and get-out-the-vote campaigns cost labor at least $9 million and were thus worth that much to the Carter-Mondale ticket. Adding the communications to union membership conservatively valued in excess of $2 million, the total climbs to $11 million.[12] Herbert Alexander, professor of political science at the University of Southern California and executive director of the Citizens' Research Foundation, puts the comparable total for the 1980 presidential campaign in excess of $15 million.[13]

Several managers and scholars of corporate PACs are convinced that corporate PACs will expand these campaign roles. Edwin Epstein, a distinguished observer of the corporate PACs, has noted:

> As labor has so well demonstrated for years, PACs provide an ideal way of coordinating within a company a wide range of grass-roots political activities that make use of human and other organizational resources found in a corporation and that are therefore so valuable in an election campaign. In the 1980s we are likely to find much greater corporate efforts to increase political participation by employees, shareholders and even retirees. The result could be a more comprehensive and extensive electoral involvement by members of the business community than we have seen in the past.[14]

The argument is another expression of the "developmental" theory of PACs: that a greater range of activities will come with maturity. It remains to be seen, of course, what corporations and membership organizations will do in the 1980s. Moreover, it is not certain that organized labor can sustain an established role that has always depended on the premise that the registrations and election-day votes its activities generate would be solidly behind the positions and candidates of labor. Recent elections, especially the one in 1980, indicate that the premise may not be as reliable as it once was.

It should be emphasized that these functional linkages—whether to voter mobilization or lobbying—are possible because the PACs support the political goals of their parent organizations. The PAC is separate from its parent for lobbying, mobilization, and fund-raising purposes, but not for mapping political goals and strategies. Even a PAC without a parent—an unaffiliated PAC—often achieves a lobbying or mobilization linkage with activists in another grass-roots group or organization. For affiliated PACs, the linkage is the result of the parent organization's articulation of a community of interest; for unaffiliated PACs, it springs from a discovered community of interest in an issue or ideology.

* * *

If it is often difficult to generalize about the two major American parties, it is even more intimidating to try to generalize about the 3,400 PACs active in national politics. They represent a vast array of groups and organizations, which in turn represent an enormous variety of industries, professions, interests, concerns, and issues. They differ widely in their political knowledge, sophistication, and confidence, and they bring many different kinds and magnitudes of resources to the political arena. This diversity of structure and function will become even more apparent as we turn now to examine their organizational lives.

5
INTERNAL LIVES AND POLITICS

The internal, private life of the political action committee is obviously more obscure than its public, reported activities. Indeed, the registration requirements of federal statutes and the Federal Election Commission require the PACs to divulge very little of their organization and operations. Nor do most journalists concern themselves with such matters. The contributions and campaign activities of the PACs are the big story.

Worse perhaps than the absence of full and detailed knowledge of the organizational life of the PACs are the mythologies that fill the vacuum. It is not uncommon for political critics to deny that the PACs have any autonomous life and to claim—depending on their point of view—that corporate or labor PACs are the subservient creatures of corporate or labor sponsors. As seductive as that myth may be, it is not easy to sustain. Even though PACs are servants of the political goals and policies of their parent organizations, they have organizational lives of their own that vary considerably from PAC to PAC. In that seeming paradox rests a basic truth about the organizational lives of PACs.

The Decision to Have a PAC

Except for the unaffiliated PACs, each PAC has a parent or founding organization behind it. That relationship is in many ways a critical one for a PAC, and in no way is it more apparent than in the initial decision whether to establish a PAC. We can learn a great deal about PACs by exploring the incidence of PACs among various kinds of organizations and the reasons for founding or not founding a PAC.

The case of labor is the simplest. Virtually every major national (or "international") labor union in the United States has a political action committee, as does labor's great umbrella organization, the AFL-CIO. The growth of labor PACs from 224 in 1976 to 380 in 1982 was relatively modest (where else would a growth rate of 70 percent in six years be called modest?) because very few unions remained to convert to the PAC movement. Most of the smaller unions with PACs were affiliated with the AFL-CIO and could consider themselves represented by its Committee on Political Education. Within organized labor, therefore, there is no questioning the desirability of PACs. They are time-honored and legitimate avenues of political activity, and neither individual workers nor the labor movement can consider individual campaign contributions a feasible alternative to collective action.

At the other extreme, in the case of the membership associations—the "trade, health, and membership" category of the FEC—it is difficult to calculate the incidence of PACs if for no other reason than the difficulty in calculating the size of the potential universe. The most authoritative source reports 14,000 nonprofit associations in the United States in 1979,[1] but that total includes a number of unlikely candidates for PACs: hobby associations, Greek-letter societies, hereditary associations, and athletic organizations. Eliminating such categories leaves a total of 10,000 or 11,000, and the 628 PACs in this category in 1982 therefore represent less than 10 percent of the potential.

Although there is little systematic scholarship on the association PACs, most observers agree that PACs are far more common among the larger than the smaller associations. They also agree that the greatest barrier to their founding is statutory. Trade associations may solicit the executive and administrative personnel of member corporations only with the consent of those corporations, and each member corporation may approve only one solicitation a year. To avoid choosing among a number of contenders, and often to protect the solicitations of their own corporate PACs, many corporations routinely deny all such requests. Consequently, trade association PACs tend to be found primarily in associations with individual (e.g., Realtors PAC) or smaller corporate members (e.g., the Associated Builders and Contractors PAC). Associations of major corporations such as the American Petroleum Institute and the Iron and Steel Institute, on the other hand, tend not to have PACs.[2]

The case of the corporate PACs is by far the most instructive, both because of their rapid growth in the late 1970s and because we know far more about them.[3] Corporations seem to decide whether or not to have a PAC depending on two chief characteristics of the corporation: its size and its position vis-a-vis government policy. First, the large corporations are most apt to have PACs. As of 1970, more than 40 percent of *Fortune*'s top 500 corporations had PACs, but only a bit more than 8 percent of the next 500 did.[4] This relationship of size to PAC is not hard to explain: larger corporations have greater resources and more employees from whom to solicit, and they are more likely to have a separate and professionally staffed public or governmental affairs unit, and a Washington office or representative. Second, the founding of a PAC appears to be related to the extent of government regulation and influence that the corporation is subject to. As Bernadette Budde, director of political education for BIPAC and one of the best-informed observers of corporate PACs, has put it:

> The more regulated an industry, the more likely it is to have a political action committee. As the government moves closer to partnership with an industry, the result of that liaison is a PAC, mothered by industry, but unmistakably sired by government.[5]

And so it is that one finds many and powerful PACs in the various energy industries, while there are relatively fewer in the apparel, furniture, publishing, and toiletries industries.

These two variables, however, by no means explain all of the decisions on establishing corporate PACs. Individual corporations must evaluate the advantages and propriety of having a PAC. Those who decide "yes" tend to see advantages in a PAC for their Washington representation, feel confident in an active social and political role, and also have leadership with strong ideological feelings about politics and the role of government. Individual or personal considerations may enter the decision as well. To some extent, a PAC gets both executives and Washington representatives "off the hook" in responding to repeated requests for individual contributions. (Having a PAC permits them to say, "I gave at the office.") Beyond these considerations are the less tangible ones. PACs are in vogue, and they appear to create political advantages, however indefinable. Other corporations have them, and a corporation without one may have a vague feeling that it is missing an opportunity or, worse, lacking in the ability to innovate.[6]

The considerations on the negative side of the ledger include a fear of public disapproval of the active political role, and fear as well of a PAC's potential for causing conflict and disagreement within the corporation's management. In the words of Irving S. Shapiro, then the chairman of the board of DuPont:

> My personal feeling is that the public has learned to tolerate labor's political action committees, but I'm not at all convinced it will tolerate the same thing from business.[7]

Finally, many corporate executives have concluded, in a simple cost-benefit analysis, that PACs are more trouble than they are worth, that the political advantages are just not as tangible as might appear at first glance. Many corporations figure they bear 50 cents to 75 cents in administrative and overhead costs for every political dollar their PACs raise. Thus many corporations simply prefer either no campaign role or action through the PAC of a trade association. The latter option ensures, among its advantages, anonymity for the corporation and much less publicity and political conflict for everyone concerned.

The origins of unaffiliated PACs are an entirely different matter. Some originate as a spin-off of an issue or ideological movement. Some have their roots in membership organizations that do not wish to establish PACs or whose PACs fail to satisfy part of the clientele. (The Gun Owners of America PAC apparently was born out of disappointment with the National Rifle Association's Victory Fund.) There is a substantial element of individual entrepreneurship in the founding of many of them. An individual or a small group of individuals, usually experienced in Washington generally and in campaigns or public policy specifically, senses a political opportunity, either a role ready for the taking or potential contributors ready for the organizing. Many of the unaffiliated PACs, therefore, inevitably appear to be extensions of the egos and enthusiasms of their leadership.[8]

Participation and Fundraising

As might be expected, different kinds of PACs solicit funds in different ways. The unaffiliated PACs have no alternative to solicitation through the mails, a mode of solicitation made far more effective by the development of machinery to compile and maintain lists of prospects and to print letters to them. The owners or masters of the lists, such as Richard Viguerie of the new right, thus assume a central role in the solicitations. The membership associations of various kinds solicit at annual conventions or other membership meetings, but they, too, rely on mail solicitation. Their membership lists are at hand, and many attach a PAC solicitation to the annual dues statement.

Solicitation methods among corporate and labor PACs are far more complicated. Labor unions are federations, and it is common for units higher in the hierarchy to set fund-raising goals or quotas for local units. For example, COPE sets quotas for its state COPEs, which have some freedom in devising ways to collect the funds. Some money is certainly collected by passing the hat at local, district, or statewide meetings. Some is collected not as contributions but as "profit" in raffles, parties, dinners, dances, or other forms of entertainment. After the 1980 elections, the AFL-CIO tried to promote the use of the "checkoff" system for collecting contributions in the local unions—that is, direct solicitation followed by regular and automatic deduction of the contributions from the paycheck. The method has obvious advantages for the union: larger, predictable contributions and systematic record-keeping. But unless the employer has a payroll deduction system for its own PAC, the checkoff can be won only through collective bargaining.

In the languishing economy of 1982 and 1983, the checkoff was not a high priority in collective bargaining for most unions, at least not one they would be willing to strike over. (The checkoff is, to be sure, easy for unions to install for their *own* employees.)

The corporate PACs usually approach their executive, administrative, and management employees with a letter of solicitation from the company's chief executive officer, often followed up with group meetings and presentations. They differ on the question of one-on-one solicitation; many use it, but some worry about its coercive implications. Some find a middle tack by using a peer rather than a supervisor as the solicitor. But whatever the form, virtually all corporate PAC managers are convinced that some form of personal solicitation is necessary. A few corporate PACs also build their solicitation campaigns around a low-key political event, such as an appearance by a candidate, public official, or party personage. Approximately two of every three corporate PACs use the payroll deduction plan.

Corporate and labor PACs are legally permitted to solicit beyond their management and member clienteles, but they rarely do so. Corporate PACs may solicit the corporation's stockholders, but probably well less than 20 percent of them do so. Those that have done so report unsatisfactory results (i.e., a response of a few percent); the chief exception appears to be a small number of corporations whose stock is held by a small number of large stockholders.[9] Moreover, both corporate and union PACs have twice-a-year crossover privileges in mail solicitations; that is, the corporate PAC may solicit its hourly workers and the union PAC may solicit management workers. Very very few corporations have done so; they are probably very small, family-held corporations with a strong sense of labor-management community. Apparently no labor PAC has ever solicited management. On either side the enterprise is unpromising—unsympathetic respondents, the inability to use personal solicitation, the unavailability of payroll deduction, and the need for an independent custodian of funds (usually a bank) to keep identities of contributors and noncontributors secret.[10]

Contributions to the PAC go into a PAC treasury (a "separate segregated fund"), from which a governing body makes disbursements. A few PACs, however, through a process of earmarking, permit the contributor to designate the party or candidate who will receive the contribution. The PAC then forwards the gift, making it clear that the money was raised through the good offices of the PAC. Only a few PACs are enthusiastic about earmarking, but one has made it a way of life. The Council for a Livable World (CLW) solicits by mail and suggests earmarking by recommending a set of candidates in the letter of solicitation. The contributor gives to one or more by check sent to the CLW. But the CLW is an unaffiliated PAC, and earmarking is not regarded enthusiastically among the PACs with parent organizations. PAC managers believe it denies the collective purpose of a PAC and may put them in the embarrassing position of forwarding contributions to candidates they oppose. Critics claim also that individuals can contribute the maximum amounts to a candidate and then "exceed" the limit with a contribution to a PAC earmarked for the same candidate. All that notwithstanding, surveys of corporate PACs indicate that 25 to 35 percent of them permit earmarking.[11]

The question of how many contributors engage in important political activity through PACs is more than a matter of mere curiosity. Corporate PACs report wildly divergent participation rates among administrative and management personnel. There are reports of participation rates that exceed 90 percent, and yet some well-run PACs report participation rates below 10 percent.[12] One survey of corporate PACs reports an average participation rate of 34 percent; another shows a median and modal response in the 10 to 25 percent range, and a third finds that 33 percent of solicited employees gave.[13] Those varying percentages reflect in part the fact that some PACs seek contributors more aggressively than others do. But in greater part they reflect different denominators in the percentage calculations.

PACs that solicit a limited segment of top management show much higher participation rates because participation is more widespread among the better paid. Those who solicit all management employees they legally can show smaller rates of participation and smaller average contributions, but larger revenue totals (see Table 5–1). Thus the percentages are not comparable, and as PACs grow and extend the range of their solicitations, their strength may even be attested to by falling rates of participation that reflect a broader base of support. These differences aside, we can estimate that corporate PACs that solicit most or all of management receive contributions from about 10 to 20 percent.

What about the size of average contributions to the PACs? In 1976, all PACs with receipts of more than $100,000 got 87 percent of their total (about $30.9 million) in sums of $100 or less; even corporate

Table 5-1
Rates and Sizes of Contributions to Corporate PACs, 1978

	Number of Managerial Employees Solicited			
	14-200	205-467	480-1,342	1,400-11,400
Participation rate, %	51	34	31	20
Average contribution	$142	$140	$124	$84
Average amount raised	$8,790	$16,771	$36,692	$73,053

Source: Survey of Public Affairs Council, reported in *PAC News* of July 27, 1979. (These data are apparently for the two-year electoral cycle.)

PACs received 66 percent in such small amounts. The median contribution thus was clearly well below $100, especially for labor PACs.[14] That calculation also squares with repeated reports from the PACs that average or median contributions are in the $25, $50, or "less than $100" ranges, and with the most recent survey of corporate PACs that reports an average annual contribution of $80.[15]

Federal statutes require that contributions to PACs be voluntary. But on this point an aura of disbelief pervades much of the writing on the PACs. Any number of observers, including some in Congress, think that corporate executives compel contributions to their PACs, and it is not hard to come by similar allegations of labor coercion in the local union halls or on the local job. Even if one had the power to command evidence and compel testimony, it would not be easy to evaluate such charges. For one thing, it is not easy to say exactly what coercion is. Is it repeated, persistent solicitation? Is it in the bringing of peer pressure? (If it is, one must conclude that much of charitable solicitation in America is "coercive," and that coercion is an integral part of American voluntarism.)

Perhaps it is sufficient to say that neither the FEC nor an American court has been convinced by any of the charges of coercion brought before them.[16] Certainly there is no evidence—or even any suggestion—of widespread or systematic coercion in the raising of PAC contributions. The fear and the allegations are voiced most frequently about corporate PACs, perhaps because of the availability of promotion and salary sanctions. Most corporate PACs, however, go out of their way to avoid any suggestion of coercion; letters of solicitation and covering letters from chief executive officers usually contain very explicit affirmations of the voluntary nature of the contribution. Furthermore, contribution percentages in the range of 10, 20, or 30 percent are hardly consistent with the coercion theories.

Internal Decisionmaking

A PAC is generally about as simple in organizational form as an organization can be in the late twentieth century. It need not be incorporated, have a written charter, or have any kind of representative or participatory structure. In short, federal statutes require only that PACs be sufficiently organized to account for their money and make reports to the FEC. With so little statutory regulation to constrain them and no regulation to "open" them to the participation of donors or members, the corporations, unions, and associations that set up PACs may control and dominate them if they wish.[17]

Most PACs do in fact have simply written by-laws that specify the creation, composition, and powers of the decision-making body or bodies that act on behalf of the PAC. Most, too, outline the methods and even the criteria for making contributions to candidates. In corporate and association PACs, the governing body usually has eleven or fewer members; there are usually more in union PACs. The trustees of corporate PACs are largely drawn from middle and upper-middle management; those of labor PACs are elected officials and representatives. In both cases they are representative in appropriate ways. The corporate PAC may represent different divisions and plant locations, different levels of management, even different political party loyalties. Larger national labor PACs, on the other hand, must represent various affiliated unions, regions, skills, and industry connections.

Power and authority in the PACs usually reflect the decisionmaking and patterns of authority in the parent organization. In corporate PACs, the chairman of the board, the president, or the designated chief executive officer most often selects the members of the governing board or committee of the PAC. In some instances he may also have the right to approve or disapprove disbursal decisions. The leadership of association PACs is usually chosen by the elected boards or officers of the association; the PAC leadership may be found right on the association's board. Even when corporate or association PACs provide for "members"—usually the contributors—those members rarely have any formal voice in the running of the PAC. Labor PACs are likely to be governed by officials or representatives chosen by the union membership. In the unaffiliated PACs, power tends to be highly centralized, in small, full-time staffs, with little constraint from boards and donors.

In reality, though, there is not as much difference between the governing of corporate and labor PACs as their formal arrangements might suggest. That is to say, there is less centralized authority in corporate PACs and more in union PACs than formal structures provide. Looking at the most important decisions of PACs—decisions about their campaign contributions—as an indication, most PACs (except the unaffiliated ones) strike similar balances between central authority and donor or member influence. They all reflect the major initiating role of the PAC managers and political technocrats on the one hand, and yet they must all be sensitive to the political demands and pressures they feel further down in the organizational hierarchy.

In corporate PACs the governing body of the PAC, or a disbursement committee it creates, makes the allocations to candidates. It gathers information, discusses PAC strategy, receives the suggestions of contributors, and may even interview the supplicant candidates. Some PACs have crafted formal and very explicit statements of procedure and criteria for contributions. The guidelines of the Honeywell Employees Political Action Committee (HEPAC) first set out the philosophic characteristics HEPAC seeks in candidates and then turn to operating criteria, among which, for example, are the following:

—Priority will be accorded to candidates in districts or states in which contributors to the PAC are located.

—Support of candidates in primaries will be considered as well as in general elections. Where there is an actively contested primary with more than one qualified candidate, supporting funds may be provided in order to assist more than one candidate to present their qualifications to the voters.

—Only under unusual conditions will this PAC make any contributions to help a candidate retire a debt which he may have incurred during a recent election.

Inevitably, the company's specialists in public or governmental affairs will be involved with the PAC and its decisions. Many of them function as the PAC manager or its secretary or treasurer.

Similarly, the Washington representative of the corporation wields considerable power in PAC matters. Some PACs are even run out of the corporations' Washington offices. Clark MacGregor, former member of Congress and former chairman of the Nixon campaign committee, chairs the political action committee of United Technologies Corporation in Washington while also serving as the company's senior vice-president. Yet not all PACs want their decisions made in Washington offices. They may be willing to integrate PAC strategy with the organization's legislative strategy, but they do not necessarily want to be its captive. As Maxwell Glen, a reporter for the *National Journal,* has pointed out:

> . . . most PAC members are not from Washington, and in deference to them, many PACs have tried to dilute the power of Washington representatives on their boards, sometimes reducing them to non-voting status, and virtually all the Washington-based trade associations, labor organizations and ideological PACs saturate their boards with local officials.[18]

The very nature of labor, association, and unaffiliated PACs as national organizations produces centralization. For example, labor's PACs—at least those active in federal elections—tend to have a hierarchical structure in which there is a pyramiding of responsibility and authority from the local to the national level. The enormous influence of Alexander Barkan, the long-time former director of COPE, reflected that organizational centralization as well as his own strength of personality. (In some PACs in the labor movement, such as the teachers' National Education Association, control over allocations is more decentralized.) The unaffiliated PACs are the most centralized in decisionmaking. Although they may have advisory councils and boards, one person or a small number of persons tend to make their important decisions.

In this entire process, donors or contributors play no formal decisionmaking role. That is not to say that they are or can be ignored.

Union members participate in the endorsement process, and they select directly or indirectly the union officials and representatives who make the decisions. For their part, a number of corporate PACs have tried to involve their contributors (or "members") in the business of the PAC. Devotion to contributor "input" is widespread among the corporate PACs, and newsletters, annual reports, and pleas for suggestions abound. The requests for "input" and the streams of "feedback" serve primarily to reinforce the contributors and to secure both their loyalty and their future contributions. But participation of this sort by contributors is not without its practical consequences. Some PAC managers freely admit that it forces on them a somewhat more diffuse and even bipartisan disbursal strategy. In the words of Clark MacGregor as he explains the goals of United Technologies' PAC:

> "To elect a more business-oriented and national defense-conscious Congress . . . and to improve our relationship with the congressmen and senators from areas where we have plants and people." But the goals sometimes are in conflict.
> "We frequently find people [in UT plants] urge us to support an incumbent or a challenger whose philosophy may not accord with our long-range objectives." Usually, he said, the PAC abides by their recommendation.[19]

Corporate, association, and union PACs must respect local views within the organization on local campaigns. It is a very rare PAC that will support a local congressional candidate over the opposition of local contributors. Despite the formal centralization of their by-laws, the local constituency of contributors that cannot be ignored is an intractable consideration in PAC decisions.[20]

The question of PAC accountability is closely related to this issue of the locus of authority. Although, as we have seen, the mechanisms of internal democracy are much more common within labor and its PACs than within American corporations and trade and professional associations, there are no real traditions of formal accountability among PACs, and what informal accountability exists depends largely on two mechanisms. First, the presence and responsibility of the parent organization, the web of relationships and loyalties it has developed, enforce a sensitivity to community and clientele on its PAC. The PAC cannot escape the parent's need to protect its interests and reputation. (Obviously, the unaffiliated PAC is not so constrained.) Second, the donor holds the sanction of "exit" over the PAC—that is, the freedom not to give the next time. Just how great that implicit threat of withdrawal is, no one knows; there appears to be no systematic evidence on the rate of, or reasons for, nonrenewal of PAC contributions.[21]

PACS IN THE AMERICAN POLITICAL SYSTEM

Not even the farsighted men who wrote the American Constitution expected the growth of popular democracy and the political organizations that would accompany it. Their writings suggest the inevitability of legislative caucuses and general groups of interests ("factions"), but little more. Neither parties nor interest groups as we know them today are mentioned, even hinted at, in the Constitution. The polity that the men of Philadelphia created, limited in suffrage and hedged about with devices of indirect representation, was years away in philosophy and time from the direct popular democracy of the twentieth century.

As the electorate expanded in the early nineteenth century with the elimination of property qualifications for voting, the political parties began their development as something more than legislative caucuses. Party organization sprang up in the local constituencies, and in 1832 the Democrats held the first representative, national party convention to nominate Andrew Jackson. It was by combining party leadership with the presidential office that Jackson became the first popularly chosen president and established the presidency as a position of popular leadership.

The electorate continued to grow throughout the nineteenth and early twentieth centuries, through successive waves of immigration and through gradual elimination of limits on black and female suffrage. By the 1920s, the limited, indirect democracy of the Founding Fathers had developed into mass, popular democracy with virtually universal suffrage. Simultaneously, the political parties became the instrument by which the popular majorities were organized behind limited numbers of candidates in elections and party programs in legislatures.

It is therefore no exaggeration to think of the early years of this century as something of a golden age for the major parties. They were stable and well established—the younger of them, the Republican party, was founded before the Civil War. They had established control of nominations for public office, not only for the presidency and Congress but for the myriad of other offices in the states and localities.

Campaigns for public office were party campaigns; parties manned the door-to-door canvassing, the election rallies, and the voter mobilization on election day. Within American legislatures, party loyalty and discipline prevailed to an extent not known today.

Much of this ascendancy was possible because the parties controlled the main incentives to political activity, especially patronage. Much, too, was possible because the uneducated, politically unsophisticated new electorates depended heavily on the simplified cues and labels that the parties afforded. It was a splendid matching of the times and the institution—the party was ideally suited for a mass politics in which low levels of information, ideology, and political awareness were the rule and in which, in fact, large numbers of new voters were first becoming aware of American life and institutions.

By the middle of the present century, however, the political parties had begun to decline in strength and importance. Their organizations lost vitality, and they could no longer discipline their members in American legislatures. Loyalty to them began to diminish, and Americans began to vote more selectively and independently.[1] Politically active Americans,[2] better informed than ever about politics, increasingly sought other avenues than the parties for their issue-centered activity. At the same time, a new breed of experts, drawing on new knowledge and technologies, began to assume the parties' old roles in campaigns, but at the price of having to raise large sums of cash for the new nonparty politics. PACs, political organizations dealing both in cash and selectivity in issues, quite easily grew and came to maturity in such a political environment.

Four Kinds of PACs

Given the complexity and variety of American politics, it is natural that PACs have developed in more than one direction. Indeed, there really is no such thing as a "single PAC movement." There are a number of kinds of PACs and a number of PAC "movements," and we can best sort them out by thinking of four main types of PACs. They reflect the very important and fundamental differences among PACs in what they do and how they do it, in what assets they command and how they mobilize them, and in the clients and constituents they energize.

Obviously, categorizing political institutions inevitably involves creating aggregate portraits or "ideal" types that very few individual examples can meet in every detail or characteristic. The types are better thought of as composites of modal characteristics whose truth and validity lie in their ability to describe general patterns rather than in their ability to depict individual PACs exactly.

The four ideal types of PACs—the money-channelers, the quasi-parties, the issue brokers, and the personal PACs—are defined not by internal or organizational characteristics but by their external activities, goals, and links to other political activities (see Table 6–1). Nonetheless, they coincide to a considerable degree with the categories of nonparty political committees the FEC uses in its reports. As we have seen, those categories derive from the presence (or absence) and the nature of the PAC's parent organization. The FEC categories include the unaffiliated PACs and five kinds of connected PACs: those of unions, corporations, associations, cooperatives, and corporations without stock. The degree of "match" or "fit" between these types— based on activities—and the FEC categories suggests a fundamental, perhaps even obvious, truth about PACs: they are to a considerable extent shaped by the goals, assets, and personnel of their parent organizations, or by the absence of them.

The *money-channelers* among the PACs operate in the classic ways of the campaign contributor: they raise money and give it to candidates. Theirs is the least innovative role in campaign politics; they do,

Table 6-1
Characteristics of Four Types of PACs

Types of PACs	Parent Organization	Dominant Form of Campaign Spending	Strategy of Campaign Spending	Linkage to Mobilization of Voters	Linkage to Legislatures (Lobbying)	Congruent FEC Categories
Money-Channelers	Heavily corporations, associations	Cash contributions to candidates	Heavily to incumbents	Little	Much	1. Corporate 2. Trade, health, membership
Quasi-Parties	Heavily labor unions	Cash contributions to candidates	Mixed to incumbents and to challengers	Much	Much	1. Labor
Issue Brokers	Some associations, none in many cases	Mix of cash contributions and independent expenditures	Heavily to challengers	Some	Some	1. Unaffiliated 2. Some membership
Personal PACs	None (except personal organization of founder)	Cash contributions to candidates	Dictated by political and ideological goals of founder	None	Varies greatly	1. Unaffiliated

somewhat more efficiently, only what campaign contributors have always done. They have often developed the legislative linkage to new heights of effectiveness, reflecting directly and powerfully the policy goals of the parent organization. Although the money-channeler may be found among association PACs, it is most common among those corporate PACs that solicit top management, receive a steady stream of substantial contributions via payroll deductions, and allocate those receipts without fuss or fanfare to candidates in ways that further their corporation's political commitments.

The *quasi-party* PACs are the PACs of the greatest scope. They are campaign contributors, but also have well-developed linkages to the mobilization of their members and to lobbying activities. More than any of the other PACs, the range of their activities most closely approaches that of the political parties. These PACs endorse candidates and set an agenda of issues in the campaign, and they try to organize their members into a cohesive electorate that accepts the name of the PAC or its parent organization as an object of voting loyalty. Thus they reach for the symbolic power in electoral politics that traditionally only the parties commanded. The labor PACs have long been the classic quasi-parties, but quasi-party PACs are also found among the membership PACs (e.g., the Political Victory Fund of the National Rifle Association).[3]

The *issue brokers* are the PACs of issues and ideological purity. The depth of their commitment to an issue or to a cluster of issues prevents them from making the pragmatic compromises necessary for achieving the broader appeal and clienteles, or the legislative influence, of the money-channelers and quasi-parties. Many of them go their own way in the campaign with separate campaigns of independent expenditures, and those that do give directly to candidates often support challengers rather than incumbents. Some of the issue brokers are based on membership organizations, but many are not, and parent membership organizations are generally little more than movements built around the issue or issues in question. That is, unlike most of the money-channelers and all of the quasi-parties, issue brokers usually have no parent organization with a separate life and function. NCPAC has been their most celebrated example in recent years, but others have devoted themselves to such specific issues as the environment, abortion, and disarmament.

Finally, the *personal* PACs are those organized around a founder or patron—the Congressional Club of Jesse Helms, for example, or the PACs maintained by Edward Kennedy, Walter Mondale, Robert Dole, and Speaker Thomas "Tip" O'Neill. As a type, they are least like the other PACs. They exist primarily to further the causes and/or political career of their founder—whether it is the triumph of an ideology (the

Helms case) or the securing of a legislative majority (O'Neill PAC) or the quest for the presidency (the Kennedy and Mondale cases and, some would argue, the Helms case as well). There is no parent organization as such; the loyalty here is to the founder and his political fortunes. In some states the personal PAC is the chosen device of contestants for leadership positions in legislatures; their contributions to candidates serve to build legislative coalitions to support their ambitions or leadership. Generally there are few linkages to other parts of the political process—few attempts to mobilize voters and little continuing effort to influence policymaking.

PACs as an Alternative to Parties

To what extent have the PACs, or some of them, begun to pick up the activities, the "functions," that the major American parties have for so long performed? Obviously, some have done more than others. That much is perhaps clear from the decision to call some but not all of them "quasi-parties." But in justification of that label one ought to review the issue more fully. First, an illustrative anecdote:

> Only days after Rep. Leo J. Ryan, D-Calif., was shot to death in Guyana last year, 15 San Francisco business leaders began interviewing his prospective replacement.
> "We got in there earlier than the political parties did," said John A. Kochevar, manager for public affairs of the Chamber of Commerce of the United States. "We boiled it down to one candidate, who, though he may not have been the most conservative, had the best chance of winning."
> That candidate, Republican realtor Bill Royer, capitalized on Democratic dissent to win the vacant California seat in last April's special election.[4]

If the definition of electoral alternatives has been the mark of the American party, and if control of the nomination is the key to control of elections, then some PACs have begun to take a partylike role in elections.[5]

The increasing tendency of PACs to endorse candidates in addition to financing them leads to the same conclusion. The second aspect of the parties' historic mastery of electoral politics is the ability to manage the campaign, provide the resources with which it is waged, and garner the gratitude and loyalty of the successful candidate. The parties lost that monopoly long ago, and now the PACs provide a substantial part of the cash with which campaign assets are rented or purchased. The third aspect of party control in elections is in the label the candidates carry on the ballot. While the labels are those of the parties, it is not clear that they can control who uses them. The advent of the direct primary in the early years of this century began to undermine that control, and the willingness of some PACs to support candidates before or in the primaries adds to the undermining.

The party label that identifies candidates in elections is significant, however, only if there is deep loyalty to it, even dependence on it, among large numbers of voters. Then the party symbol organizes the perceptions and loyalties of voters and helps them to form and to act on an ordered picture of the political universe. It provides the great political shortcut. The golden age of the political party was sustained by the willingness of great numbers of Americans to accept and act on its recommendations. That was the foundation on which high levels of straight-ticket voting and cohesive majorities in legislatures rested.

The loyalties to single issues or issue clusters that many PACs have fostered in the 1970s and 1980s certainly match those party loyalties in intensity and dominance. Indeed, the very idea of dominance—of the loyalty that transcends other loyalties—is built into the concept of single-issue politics. But these issue clienteles hardly match the loyal party clienteles of generations ago in breadth and numbers. Quite simply, PACs do not build the extensive, inclusive appeal that the parties had and still have. PACs reach out and build coalitions only to a limited degree. Their success in raising political money seems to depend on the narrowness and specificity of the interest or issue behind the appeal. It is most strikingly so in direct mail appeals, where the most successful letters of solicitation are the ones with focused, emotional, even negative appeals. Political selectivity and specific issue concerns can apparently override even loyalty to an occupation or profession. Labor learned that in the last decade or two, and so have a number of issue-brokering PACs.

So, what of PACs and the party role? Individual PACs take over some but not all of the role of the parties. Some PACs mobilize voters and pick candidates; some try to mobilize legislatures, though only on an issue or two. Some are locked in the kind of organizational combat that typifies the competition of the parties. Instead of Democrats versus Republicans, for example, a liberal PAC, Democrats for the 80s, tilted over the airwaves with NCPAC in the early skirmishes of the 1982 senatorial campaign.[6] But no individual PACs begin to approach the totality of the party role, and in the last decade the PACs with narrowly defined issues and very specific missions have made the great leaps forward. Political selectivity in the electorate breeds fragmentation among political organizations. So, in their aggregate but uncoordinated way, the PACs do some of the things the parties no longer do. They furnish a replacement, but not a substitute, for the parties because they have found no ways to build majorities or even large minorities in the electorate. The very changes in American electoral politics that made it difficult for the parties to fill their classic roles make it even more difficult for their competitors to do so.

The New Participation

Beyond their activities in American elections and legislatures, PACs have made their mark on another aspect of American democracy. Their supporters claim the PACs have broadened the base of participation in American politics in two ways: by bringing new participants into political activity and by broadening participation in the private funding of election campaigns. The points are clearly related but just as clearly separate. In any event, the whole issue of "participation" assumes a specific salience at a time when voting as a form of political participation has been waning. The suggestion is very strongly implied that the PACs are succeeding where the parties have failed.

That the PACs serve the American democracy by bringing new participants into it is a repeated theme of their friends in Congress. Thus the praise of Representative William Frenzel, Republican of Minnesota:

> Hundreds of thousands of thoughtful Americans, not satisfied with parties, turned off on politicians, find political expression by contributing through a reference group. It may be a union, a corporation, a professional association, or an ideological group. Whatever it is, they have confidence in it. Yes, PACs are growing because people like them. They find PACs a convenient way to participate in the political processes of this Nation.[7]

The unspoken major premise, of course, is that greater participation per se is desirable. It is a populist argument, one very much in tune with the democratic hopes and assumptions of the American middle class. Commitment to that premise is evident in the alarm we show over political inactivity and the fervor with which we grasp once more the tools of direct democracy such as popular referenda.

However one arrives at an estimate, millions of Americans each year make contributions to or through PACs. In 1980, the Center for Political Studies of the University of Michigan asked a national adult sample if they had made a contribution to a "political action group" in that year. Almost 6 percent (94 of a total of 1,614, or 5.8 percent) said they had. That percentage projected onto an adult electorate of 150 million yields a figure of 8.7 million Americans.[8] Many observers would consider this collective estimate inflated, both because Americans chronically overreport their political activity and because the CPS's questions may have invited some overreporting.[9]

We can develop an alternative estimate by beginning with the approximately $140 million received in 1979–80 by all of the PACs registered with the FEC. If we assume on the basis of fragmentary evidence that state and local PACs received a somewhat smaller sum of $120 million, the resulting total for the two-year cycle is $260 million.[10] Since more was contributed in the second year of the cycle, the election year, than in the first, we can estimate all PAC receipts for 1980 at about $180 million. If we then assume an average contribution of $30, we arrived at a total of 6 million contributors; if we assume an average contribution of $50, then there were 3.6 million contributors. To move from the number of contributions to the number of contributors, we further discount these figures by 20 percent to account for repeat contributors and arrive at a range of 2.9 million to 4.8 million contributors to PACs in the election year 1980.

And who are the contributors to PACs? Are they new to political activity? Are they new even to the making of financial contributions? The hunches and convictions of observers differ greatly. Michael Malbin, one well-informed observer of the PACs, has argued that a substantial number of PAC contributors are old contributors in new guise—that is, that they are merely the individuals who used to make large individual contributions before the 1974 limits were enacted.[11] At the other extreme some of the more zealous PAC managers perceive the PACs as drawing contributors from the sloughs of political inactivity. As he was testifying before a congressional committee, Richard Berman of the Steak and Ale restaurant chain was asked to clarify a statement. Did he really mean to say that 99 percent of the contributors to his PAC had not contributed or participated in the political process?

> Correct. Have never contributed money in the political process, and many of these people felt terribly disenfranchised, and I know through personal conversations, had not participated in the voting process.[12]

Neither of these men presents concrete evidence to support his argument. If for no other reason than the average size of contributions after 1974, it seems unlikely that the great bulk of PAC contributors are displaced big spenders. Berman's thesis, on the other hand, flies in the face of what we know about PAC contributors in the 1980 elections (Table 6–2). Those data indicated that contributors to "political action groups" are better informed and more political than the average American but less so than contributors to parties and candidates. They come, in essence, from the relatively less active part of the politically active and concerned minority in the American electorate.

To understand political participation through PACs, we need also to note the nature of the participation. Some of it is not even political activity; buying a ticket in a raffle, the proceeds of which go to a PAC, a party, or a candidate, does not qualify as a political act by most standards. Even the contributory act of writing a check or giving cash to a PAC is a somewhat limited form of participation that requires little

Table 6-2
Donors to PACs, Candidates, and Parties (1980)*

Percentage who:	Donors to Groups	Donors to Candidates	Donors to Parties
Went to political meetings	20	38	43
Voted in 1980	87	93	94
Were "very much" interested in congressional election	30	47	55
Watched television news "every night"	23	35	57

Source: Center for Political Studies of the University of Michigan.

*About 60 percent of the entire adult sample reported voting in 1980, and only 7 percent said they went to political meetings.

time or immediate involvement; in a sense it buys political mercenaries who free the contributor from the need to be personally active in the campaign. It is one of the least active forms of political activity, well suited to the very busy or to those who find politics strange, boring, or distasteful.

Political activity through PACs, therefore, is a new and different kind of political activity, at least partially detached from the traditional electoral politics of parties and candidates. Except for those who earmark contributions, PAC contributors surrender control over the final destination of their dollars. Giving to PACs is giving to promote an issue or the interests of the parent organization rather than the interests of a party or candidate; it is thus an extension of interest-group politics into campaign politics. As such, it is very much a reflection of the political selectivity of large numbers of Americans and of their desire to find avenues of political activity that relate most directly to their personal political agendas.

The Growth Curve and the Future

We have had only five elections, only two of them presidential, under the new regulatory regime. But the growth of the PACs and their contributions in that very short time has been so dramatic that it has created concern and apprehension about their future. When we think of the PACs and their activities as policy issues, we have in mind not so much their past as the future we imagine them having. The past of the PACs really *is* prelude.

It is always natural to project the continued rise of growth curves. The sharper the incline of the curve, the less likely it seems that it will level off or turn down. But in anticipating social growth of any kind we are much better off looking not at growth curves but at the influences shaping them. These influences include both internal mechanisms of growth—the awakening and publicity factors, the "everyone-is-doing-it" psychology, and the dynamics of the diffusion of any idea—and a series of factors external to the PACs.

The major factors external to the PACs are readily apparent: the legal climate, the parties, and the general political environment. We have already seen how the legal environment changed very sharply in the 1970s, and how the changes created, intentionally and unintentionally, a series of opportunities for the PACs. Much of the growth of the past six or seven years has come from a seizing of those opportunities. By now much of that phase is certainly over; many major organizations have decided either to have PACs or not to have them. If we assume that the legal environment will not become more favorable for the PACs—and that seems a safe assumption—then one very strong stimulus to the development of PACs has substantially run its course. Obviously, any restrictions added to the legal environment would inhibit their growth.

Moreover, it is difficult to see that the party environment will open new opportunities for PAC growth. Certainly, the parties will not continue their decline indefinitely. There are signs that the decline is leveling off and that the parties have begun to define and hold a new, though reduced role for themselves in American politics. The growth of independents in the American electorate has stopped, for example, and the decline of party cohesion in Congress seems to have been arrested. There is even some sign of party revival. The Republican national campaign committees raised more money in the 1980 elections than a set of national party committees has ever raised. And now the Democratic National Committee has begun, however belatedly, to chart the same course. It is in the best American tradition of "joining 'em if you can't beat 'em," and PACs may well face new competition from the parties in raising and contributing campaign dollars.

PAC growth will continue to reflect the politics of the times. It does not appear that reliance on media-based campaigns will change or that they will slake their almost insatiable thirst for cash. Nor does it seem likely that an active, issue-oriented American electorate will soon abandon its selectivity about candidates or issues. So, two of the great stimuli for growth of PACs appear likely to continue in force. However, the current conservative resurgence in the nation and the states may well remove some very powerful PAC-developing influences. If the Reagan administration's policies of deregulation and devolving greater responsibilities to the states succeed, one fundamental influence on the growth of national PACs will diminish: the threat or reality of entanglements with the federal government.

And what of internal influences within the PACs, their parent organizations, and their clienteles? They are the most difficult to predict or project. Will organizations be willing to bear increasing overhead costs for PACs? Is there some point at which some organizations will conclude that PACs are more costly and troublesome than they are worth? To what extent is there potential for the recruitment of new donors to the PACs? Does the publicity the PACs have recently received drive away potential donors, or does it increase contributions by making PACs more visible and significant and by encouraging the growth of PACs as a new and successful way to political influence? To ask such questions is almost to confess an absence of answers. Perhaps one can only say that the growth of PACs—in number and in receipts—seems bound up with the larger question of the growth of campaign spending and with the willingness of Americans to contribute larger and larger sums of money to campaign politics.

Unless we shift substantially to public funding of campaigns, individual contributors remain central to any estimates of the future of PACs, since all private campaign finance originates with individual contributions. In many ways the most striking fact in American campaign finance has been the persistence, despite the reforms of the 1970s, of individual contributors as the dominant force in campaign finance. They continue to provide almost two-thirds of candidate receipts, and the growth of their contributions in the early 1980s almost matches that of PAC contributions. The future growth of PACs seems to depend very directly on the ability of PACs to persuade many of those individual contributors that the way to their political goals is through organized, rather than personal, giving.

THE POINTS OF CONCERN

The debate over political action committees is largely a debate over their impact on the American political system and on American democracy. On the face of it, there is little that is intrinsically wrong about them. They and their contributors engage in legal political activity that is moreover protected by the First Amendment's guarantees of freedom of speech and association. The controversy over PACs—and the movement to regulate or reform them—is about the impact they have on the nation's democratic politics. Moreover, any assessment of that kind is only in part a question of political fact and reality. It also is a question of the interpretation and evaluation of that reality, and in that realm one quickly moves beyond fact and into basic issues of values and desiderata.

Much of the debate over PACs and their growth develops a relatively small number of themes. Often the debate is over campaign finance generally and only partially about PACs in particular. It is difficult to separate concerns about the PACs from more general concerns about the financing of American electoral politics, and it would be a mistake to try. We can, however, separate the issues that touch PACs directly from those that appear to do so indirectly or only tangentially. After looking at the latter briefly and somewhat summarily, we will explore four central issues that deal directly with the PACs and their consequences for American democracy.

The Tangential Issues

First among the tangential issues is the question of the *amounts of money spent* in American election campaigns. By a usually unspecified standard, the cost of campaigns is said to be too high. The problem is in finding the appropriate standard. It is easy to agree upon a market standard for a diamond or a cotton shirt, but none exists for campaign finance. Nor are cross-national comparisons really valid in view of the great differences in political systems and political traditions among the democratic nations of the world.[1] Generally the most appropriate criteria appear to be those of American advertising costs because they, too, involve persuasion carried out largely in the mass media. By that standard the $1.2 billion spent on all campaigns in 1980 just about equals the advertising costs for toiletries and toilet goods in that year and is dwarfed by the $31 billion spent in 1980 on radio, newspaper, and television advertising.[2]

There are, to be sure, a few independent souls who argue that we do not spend enough on American campaigns. (The argument is more often heard concerning the presidential campaigns, on which there is a tight spending lid if the candidates accept public funding.) Walter K. Moore, who was an officer of the National Committee for an Effective Congress, one of the oldest of the liberal ideological PACs, invoking a standard from consumption totals rather than advertising, comments:

That we spend less on federal campaigns than on women's nail polish or garden hoses is as important an indictment of the political system as the fund-raising scandals associated with Watergate. They are, after all, merely parts of the same problem.[3]

Or as Herbert Alexander points out:

. . . fund raising has not kept pace with the rising costs of campaigning. The rise in the costs of television time has far outstripped the consumer price index.[4]

In general, campaign money remains a relatively scarce resource. When the unknown candidate lacks seed money for a campaign, or when an able candidate without a personal fortune is at a competitive disadvantage, it is possible to view either the supply of campaign money or its distribution (or both) as inadequate.

Much of the rhetoric of dissatisfaction with PACs is caught up with a second question: that of *the so-called special interests.* PACs are subjected to the same criticisms that interest groups have experienced through most of American history: that they represent the special interests and make it difficult to find or promote the common or public interest. It is the argument of the many against the few, the community against the self, the whole against the part. As such, of course, it rests on a belief in an identifiable public interest independent of the sum of special or particular interests.

The search for the public interest in the academy and the press has been a long and not altogether successful one.[5] Nor have we found much easier the search for a consensus on what we mean by the nonpublic or special interests. Like beauty, they seem to be in the eye of the beholder: selfish interests, economic interests, narrow or minority interests, powerful interests. Indeed, "special" interests come perilously close to meaning "the interests I oppose or that oppose mine."

Perhaps it is sufficient to note that most political money is "interested" money; that is, it is given for a political purpose, in pursuit of some political goal. In a real sense, therefore, political money reflects "special" or "selfish" interests unless it has been given for nonpolitical purposes such as, for example, the winning of a lottery or the placating of a friend. If there were consensus on the goals, no political action would be necessary to secure them. Group political activity, including that of PACs, reflects rather than creates division or disagreement. Social cleavages precede and give rise to politics.

Third, and finally, among these tangential issues is that of the *tone and style of campaigning*. The campaigns of 1980 and 1982 have struck a good many observers as especially "dirty" and "negative." However, the concern may not so much be over the tone per se as it is over the heightened effectiveness of the tone now that, it is said, advertising and media experts have perfected it for political use.

Whatever one may think about the aesthetics and ethics of political advertising, it is hard to see it as a PAC issue. The substance and tactics of campaigning reflect a great many influences beyond the PACs—the use of media and advertising wisdom, sophisticated polling about candidate "images" in the electorate, the need for emotionalism in direct mail appeals, even the unflattering findings about what influences political "consumers." The one tie to PACs, of course, is in the data the Federal Election Commission keeps on independent expenditures for and against candidates. In 1980 and 1982, PAC independent spending in congressional races was heavily negative, in great part a reflection of expenditures by the National Conservative Political Action Committee. But those data say nothing about the tone or truth of those campaigns, and we have no points of reference by which we can tell how much of ordinary campaigning is similarly "negative."

The Legislative Connection

Of all the major controversies surrounding the PACs, none is as troubling to most Americans as the conversion of campaign contributions into legislative successes. It is summarized in the critical cliche about "the best Congress (or state legislature) that money can buy." Less dramatically, perhaps, the concern is that money is given to legislative candidates for some purpose and that, if the candidate wins office, the purpose of the contributor will be served. In the words of Fred Wertheimer, president of Common Cause:

There really isn't that much question about why individual special interest groups are willing to spend hundreds of thousands, even millions, of dollars on the campaigns of Congressional candidates. PACs in many cases represent an investment. The investment nature can be understood when we realize what the stakes are—government decisions that affect billions and billions of dollars. I think this can be seen when we look at the fact that most of the money goes to incumbents because incumbents hold power.[6]

The concern is limited largely to the campaign contributions of PACs, rather than those of individual contributors, because of PACs' effective ties, especially through parent organizations, to interest group lobbying.

Periodically a vote in Congress so dramatically juxtaposes contribution and legislative success that it becomes briefly a *cause célèbre* in the media and in reports of so-called public interest groups. In 1981 and 1982, it was the ill-fated attempt of the Federal Trade Commission to force used-car dealers to divulge all the defects of a car for sale on a sticker.[7] Similarly, reports persist of corporate PACs making campaign contributions to members of committees legislating on their interests. The *Washington Post*, for example, reported that in the first seven months of 1983 the forty-two members of the House Energy and Commerce Committee received a total of $1.8 million in campaign contributions, most of it from corporate PACs (such as those in oil, steel, and insurance) with direct financial stakes in the committee's decisions.[8]

Such evidence is anecdotal. It reports isolated incidents, and we have no idea how typical they are. But the fact of their existence, even if atypical, troubles many Americans. So, too, is the testimony of members of Congress to the influence of campaign money. The week after her defeat in a campaign for the Senate, Representative Millicent Fenwick wrote:

That these groups influence the voting is undeniable. "I took $58,000. They want it," was the explanation one colleague gave me for his vote, bought by a number of donations from a number of groups of similar orientation. Or consider the statement on the floor of the House by a colleague announcing his retirement: "I know why they give this to me and they know I know. If I do what they want, I feel I've been bought. If I don't, I feel . . ." he hesitated, "ungracious." I think he meant "like a cheat." He went on, "I can't do it anymore. I'm not running again."[9]

The very substantial reportage in the major newspapers and television networks of the country magnifies these concerns.

Yet there are reasons for caution in drawing firm conclusions about the generation of legislative influence through campaign contributions. In instances such as the FTC attempt to reform the used-car business, how are we to know how members who accepted car-dealer money would have voted had they received no contributions? Were those contributions intended to win converts for the car dealers, or did they reward earlier positions and votes? That is, do the votes follow the money, or does the money follow the votes? (If the money follows the votes, there is still a "legislative connection," but it is one of a different sort.) And in such instances how are we to separate the legislative effect of the campaign contributions from the effect of ordinary lobbying? The car dealers have active and vocal members in virtually every congressional district and would be a potent force in Washington even with sharply reduced levels of campaign contributions.[10]

The legislative connection can also be seen as the intersection of the political intentions of the PAC and the political position of the legislator. PACs obviously give money for the same range of goals as do individual contributors. Some pursue a general ideological goal, some are committed to a party or an issue, some are concerned with one or two specific legislative proposals, and some seek access and a friendly ear in the legislature. Unhappily, we have no way of identifying either the relative importance or specific instances of any of these goals or intentions.

Legislators also vary in their dependence on specific contributors. While that dependence results from a complicated network of factors—the size of the contribution, its relation to total campaign resources, its relationship to the voting constituency, and the looming needs of the next campaign—there is a bit more data on it. On average, each member of the House in 1981 and 1982 received 33 percent of his or her 1980 campaign funds from PACs. (All candidates for the House, including the losers, received 29 percent.) Furthermore, each member of the House received on average $196,500 for his or her 1980 campaign, of which an average of $62,500 came from PACs. Thus, a $5,000 contribution constituted 3 percent of a member's campaign resources; a $1,000 gift, about 0.5 percent. The average PAC contribution was $614, and the average winner accepted contributions from 102 PACs. PAC contributions, therefore, are widely dispersed, and very few members of Congress would seem to be politically dependent on any one or a small number of PACs.

Finally, we must put the link between campaign contributions and legislative influence in the broader context of congressional politics. Two points seem especially relevant. First, legislative incumbency is itself a shield against the pressure and sanctions of PACs. There is a lively literature on the ability of incumbents to entrench themselves firmly—possibly too firmly—in Congress.[11] They win reelection by aiding and flattering their constituents and by keeping their own names and faces visible. Incumbents also find it easier and easier to attract campaign money as their seniority places them in positions of influence. Second, the expectations of PACs, and of all campaign contributors, is only one set of pressures a member of Congress confronts. Voters in the home state or district exert theirs, and so does the party. Presidents are not without influence in Congress, particularly for members of their party. And the members themselves come to the legislative tasks with personal values, commitments, and ideologies. PACs, in other words, face hefty competition for the attention and response of the members of Congress.

Money and Election Victory

If the last issue was one of "buying" legislatures, this one concerns the "buying" of elections: the fear that money makes candidates into winners and that its absence dooms them to defeat. As with the legislative connection, the causal relationship is obscure because it is as difficult to identify the effect of any one influence in an election as it is to separate the individual determinants of a vote in Congress.

Undoubtedly the most sophisticated scholarship on the subject is that of Gary Jacobson, a professor of political science at the University of California at San Diego, who has attempted to relate the size of the vote for candidates to the amounts of money they spend in the campaign.[12] Although he found no relationship for incumbents, for challengers the greater the sums of campaign money, the greater their percentage of the two-party vote. Jacobson considered all the causal possibilities of this relationship: that more money overcomes the advantages of incumbency and maximizes the challenger's total vote, that winning challengers spend more because their prospects of winning attract more money from contributors, or that experienced, visible, charismatic challengers attract both votes and money more or less simultaneously. Jacobson concluded that the primary explanation is the first: that money enables challengers to compete effectively with incumbents. The major policy implication is clear: any system of regulation or public funding that sets the same spending levels for all candidates will work to the advantage of incumbents and the disadvantage of challengers. And the lower the spending levels, the greater the effect.

Less complicated journalistic analyses tend to follow two paths. One identifies the expensive campaigns—in 1982, particularly those funded by wealthy candidates themselves—and charts their outcomes. Depending on the selection and on the year, the score varies, but inevitably some of the big spenders win and some lose. The problem, once again, is with limited, anecdotal evidence. At the most it entitles us to conclude that "big spenders" don't always win and don't always lose—

or, in more formal scholarly language, that variations in money spent do not account for all the variations in votes garnered. The second approach, a more extensive and systematic one, is typified by two analyses of the 1982 elections reported by Patrick Caddell and by the *New York Times*.[13] Caddell reports that the Democrats won 78 percent of the "close" House elections (margins of 52 percent or less) when spending was "comparable" and only 29 percent when they were outspent by two to one or more. The *Times* computer analysis found that the Republicans won forty-two of the races in which the victors won by 55 percent or less, the Democrats forty-one. But 69 percent of these Republican winners spent at least $50,000 more than their opponents did, while only 15 percent of Democratic winners so outspent their opponents.

Such analyses deal with total receipts and spending in campaigns. The Jacobson conclusions bear on spending disparities between incumbents and challengers to which PACs may contribute. The Caddell-*New York Times* studies clarify the consequences of disparities in party resources that may in part reflect patterns of PAC giving. Both support the common wisdom that money can indeed affect election outcomes. PACs, as major sources of that money, share responsibility for its effects.

Because of its boisterous leadership, its enormous resources, its unrepentant conservatism, its negative campaigning, and its reliance on independent expenditures, the National Conservative Political Action Committee stands apart as a special case for concern. However, by the count of most observers (though not by its own), NCPAC succeeded in defeating only one of its fourteen targeted incumbent members of Congress in 1982 after boasting a far more impressive record in 1980. Again, we can conclude only that money spent in campaigns— this time money spent independently in heavily negative campaigns— does not always determine the outcome.[14]

The Balance of Power in the United States

The third major issue about PACs deals with the balance of power in American politics, and may well be the most fundamental. It revolves around the question of whether the rise of PACs works to the advantage of one set of interests in American politics and to the disadvantage of other competing interests. In terms of the conventional polarities of our politics, it is a question of whether the PACs tip the scales in favor of or against Democrats or Republicans, liberals or conservatives, labor or business. It is the issue of who gets the increments of influence that result from the growing resources of PACs.

On one level, these concerns can be addressed by pointing out that

Democrats and Republicans shared remarkably evenly in the expenditure of PAC money in the 1970s and early 1980s. To the extent that PAC money is pragmatic—and much of it is—it will continue to be allocated not to tip the scales of political power but to affirm their existing equilibrium. Democrats took the lion's share of funds in the mid-1970s; if Republican fortunes stay high, Republicans will reap the benefits in the 1980s. But the assurance of the pragmatic nature of PACs does not still all critics, especially those from organized labor:

> . . . the resources needed for achieving political influence are distributed unequally in society and . . . if we want to democratize our political system, we should avoid the distractions that take our attention away from these resources.[15]

There is no doubt about the literal facts of that argument. The affluent, by definition, have more money, and they give more of it to candidates for public office, either directly or indirectly, than do poorer people. But the real issue here is hidden in another unspoken major premise: that money or cash is the prime or overpowering political resource, and that in assessing its impact, we are justified in ignoring the distribution of countervailing or offsetting political resources. Many labor unions and PACs, for example, can command a membership loyalty and an organizational network that would be the envy of most corporate PACs. One of the great ironies of the continuing debate over PACs is that the very arguments that labor now makes about tilts in the allocation of political influence were the ones that conservatives made in the mid-1970s when faced with the superior strength of union PACs.

Scholars have never found it easy to assess the distribution of political power in the United States, and the matter cannot be settled here. The influence of PACs cannot be considered apart from the political influence their parent organizations can generate, and the influence of any group or interest in American politics cannot be fairly calculated by looking at the distribution of only one political asset, whether it is money, status, knowledge, organization, or sheer numbers. Concern about the inequality of political influence in American life has clearly motivated much of the reform of campaign finance. Many Americans have thought that the chief purpose of that legislation ought to be to place all of the contestants at a single starting line. The Supreme Court in the *Buckley* case, however, brushed aside that rationale for limiting the freedom of individuals and groups with these magisterial phrases:

> . . . the concept that government may restrict the speech of some elements of our society in order to enhance the relative voice of others is wholly

foreign to the First Amendment. . . . The First Amendment's protection against governmental abridgement of free expression cannot properly be made to depend on a person's financial ability to engage in public discussion.[16]

If legislation is not the solution to inequality, what is? The most common nonlegislative "solution" for these concerns is the pluralist argument that every temporary advantage taken in American politics by new organizations or new aggregates of influence will generate or encourage the development of countervailing power. If, for example, conservative forces stole a march on liberals with their ideological PACs, negative campaigns, and independent expenditures in 1978 and 1980, they gave rise to a whole set of liberal PACs: for example, Independent Action, PROPAC, Democrats for the 80s, and Americans for Common Sense.

The pluralists also argue that an increase in the numbers of PACs leads to greater diversity and countervailing power among them. The growth of PACs and PAC money may actually diminish the likelihood of uncontrolled PAC power by setting PAC against PAC and by spreading PAC resources more widely. The fact that the winners in House races in 1980 received contributions, on the average, from more than 100 PACs speaks eloquently to that dispersion. This picture of American politics as a self-regulating and self-equalizing mechanism, effectively at work, is a seductive one. The trouble with the pluralist faith is that, while there are surely countervailing tendencies in American politics, there is no "unseen hand" that ensures that the fullest representation will be achieved. What of the poor and the unemployed, and what of the white-collar middle class that is neither labor nor business? Because the PACs build on existing organizations, they put the unorganized at a greater disadvantage.

Responsibility and Control

To whom are the PACs responsible for their political decisions? What members or constituents set limits on their operations? Are they subject to any controls and constraints other than the freedom of their contributors to decide not to contribute anymore? For all of their obvious oligarchic tendencies, the American major parties have mechanisms of internal responsibility—caucuses, conventions, higher officials chosen by the lower ranks. They are, moreover, responsible, through their label on the ballot, to millions of voters. What then about the PACs?

First, there is little likelihood of PAC responsibility to large numbers of voters. Candidates do not carry PAC labels in the election, and it is very difficult for an opponent to pin one on during the campaign. The public disclosure of their expenditures achieves only a modest degree of visibility for only a very small number of voters. Internally, only labor PACs are subject to substantial membership control. Corporate PACs often encourage contributor opinion, and they must be sensitive to it, but they are governed by self-perpetuating bodies drawn from upper-middle management, and their decisions are intended primarily to carry out the interests of the corporation itself. The same can be said for association PACs. The constraints of the parent organization, its personnel, its reputation and public image, and its community relations are not always major, but they are stronger than the constraints on unaffiliated, nonmembership PACs. The unaffiliated PACs are the creatures of a very small number of leaders or political entrepreneurs, and their only major constraint is the need to ensure the success of the next solicitation drive.

The question of accountability is pressing partly because of the widespread belief that group leadership is often unrepresentative of group membership. Representative Jim Leach of Iowa, for example, made the point forcefully during the debate on the Obey-Railsback proposal to limit PAC spending:

> Groups seldom reflect the same collective judgment as all their members. More importantly, decisions for organizations frequently occur at the top not the bottom and the abdication of local control over funds leads to the aggrandizement of leadership power within any government channel where the organization's impact is felt. Individuals who control other people's money become power brokers in an elitist society. Their views, not the small contributors to their association, become the views that carry influence.[17]

There is an alternative formulation to Leach's: that it will be the interests of the parent organization rather than those of the small contributors that the PAC managers will pursue.

The problem of responsibility arises from the very nature of the PAC. While the political party is responsible for its activities and performance through elections and unhappy voters can defeat its candidates, PACs largely escape voter sanctions at elections. They have defined their organization and constituency in terms that have nothing to do with the local electoral district. (The strategy of liberals and Democrats, though, was clearly to make Terry Dolan and NCPAC an issue in 1982.) Furthermore, the statutes of the states provide various kinds of citizen control of and participation in the party organizations but PACs are largely run by centralized, self-perpetuating elites, checked "from below" primarily by the right of contributors to "exit."

All of these issues of accountability are heightened in the case of the unaffiliated PACs. No parent organization or membership contingent imposes constraints on them, and a small cadre of leadership is free to commit the PAC to issues very few of the contributors know of, or even share.[18] When these unaffiliated PACs spend heavily in independent expenditures, they control the final entry of those dollars into the campaign. There is not even the opportunity for the kind of voter response that is possible when candidates use funds that PACs have given them directly. To be sure, only a relatively small number of PACs and a relatively small proportion of all PAC money are involved. They are not insignificant, though, and the publicity surrounding them has given them a symbolic importance greater than their resources per se might seem to warrant.

* * *

Concerns and fears about the PACs have multiplied with their growth and increasing strength. PACs have already begun to spark a policy debate in Congress and a few state legislatures, for it is not in the American nature to leave actors and institutions in American politics to their own devices. For almost a century we have subjected the American parties to the most intense legislation and regulation known in a Western democracy. We have legislated on lobbying with a vengeance, and in the past ten years we have developed probably the most systematic and comprehensive regulation of campaign finance. Why then would we be expected to exempt the PACs from legislative scrutiny and control?

8
REFORM AND RECONSTRUCTIONS?

Reform of political finance in the United States has become a continuing enterprise, and the political action committees seem destined to be a part of it. One position in American law and politics opposes almost any legislative controls on campaigning on constitutional grounds, on the argument that such legislation inevitably places "prior restraint" on the freedom of political speech.[1] But it is not a widely held position, and while the Supreme Court has extended the coverage of the First Amendment to campaigning, it has not ruled out all restrictions on it. Within limits, then, further legislation is constitutionally permissible, and most Americans are at least willing to consider the possibility.

In addition to the constraints imposed by Supreme Court interpretations of the Constitution, there are two other major sets of limits to reform: the administrative and the political. The former largely concerns the capabilities of the Federal Election Commission; the latter involves a complex set of political realities, in Congress and the presidency and in the public at large. Taken together, these three types of constraints narrow the range of policy options considerably and define their "feasibility" and "practicality."

The Limits to Reform

Of all the limits to the reform of PACs, by far the most intractable is the Constitution of the United States as expounded by the Supreme Court. In ruling on the constitutionality of the Federal Election Campaign Act in the *Buckley* case,[2] the Court extended the protections of the First Amendment to the use of money in campaigns. Nonetheless, the Court rejected the argument for absolute constitutional protection for campaign finance. Although it struck down legislative limits on expenditures, by candidates and spenders independent of them, it upheld those on contributions. In contrast with the limitation on candidates' expenditures, the Court said, a limitation on what a group or individual can contribute "entails only a marginal restriction upon the contributor's ability to engage in free communication."[3]

In exploring the line between permissible and prohibited regulation of campaign finance, the Court weighed the interests that Congress might legitimately pursue. Over and over again the Court returned to one interest: "the governmental interest in preventing corruption and the appearance of corruption. . . ."[4] That phrase and the other variants of it in *Buckley* invite a number of comments. First, it is not very clear exactly what the Court means by "corruption." In one revealing passage it refers to the danger of permitting "unscrupulous persons and organizations to expend unlimited sums of money in order to obtain improper influences over candidates for elective office."[5] Does the Court here refer to all "big spenders," and if not, which ones? Is it possible that by "improper" influence the Court means "excessive" influence? And is it influence over candidates or influence over elected officeholders that concerns it? Second, what does the Court mean by the "appearance" of corruption? Is the regulatory power of Congress under the First Amendment directly related to the low levels of confidence that American citizens have in our parties, politicians, and candidates for office?

The justices were clearer about the interests that Congress could *not* promote. In *Buckley v. Valeo*, the Court rejected the interest in equalizing political influence:

> . . . the concept that government may restrict the speech of some elements of our society in order to enhance the relative voice of others is wholly foreign to the First Amendment. . . .[6]

It also rejected just as positively the governmental interest in reducing the costs of political campaigning. ("The First Amendment denies to government the power to determine that spending to promote one's political views is wasteful, excessive, or unwise.")[7] Obviously, the Court could not and did not run through all possible rationales for government regulation. What, for instance, of the interest of the government in maintaining relatively open access to public office for individuals without personal fortunes? What of the interest in maintaining two-party competition in the races for Congress? What, more generally (if appearances can be taken into account), of the legislative interest in maintaining confidence in the fairness and openness of American politics?

Buckley v. Valeo is a relatively recent decision, and since all of its assorted issues were decided by 6–2 or 7–1 margins, it will be modified in the near future only if some of the justices back away from its logic.[8] The Court, in fact, signaled its commitment to the direction of *Buckley* in two subsequent cases. The first was *First National Bank of Boston v. Bellotti*, a 1978 case in which it struck down a Massachusetts law forbidding a corporation to spend money in a referendum campaign on a subject that did not directly affect the corporation's economic interests.[9] In such constitutionally protected speech, the Court ruled, the legislature was "disqualified from dictating the subjects about which persons may speak and the speakers who may address a public issue."[10]

In 1981, the Supreme Court ruled on a second referendum case, this one concerning a Berkeley, California, ordinance limiting contributions to committees campaigning on referenda to $250. Even though it involved a limit on contributions rather than spending, the Court held the ordinance unconstitutional on the ground that no legitimate legislative purpose was served. Drawing a distinction between campaigns of candidates for public office and campaigns on public issues, the Court found no danger of corruption in the absence of candidates for elective public office. The integrity of referenda campaigns, the justices said, could be adequately protected by public disclosure of contributions.[11]

The constraints that the Supreme Court set on congressional action have only recently begun to trigger a reaction. In 1982, J. Skelly Wright, a senior and respected judge of the Court of Appeals for the District of Columbia, wrote a scathing commentary on the Court's position.[12] In the same year, several members of Congress began to formulate constitutional amendments that would overturn at least that part of *Buckley* that voided legislative limits on expenditures. The proposal of Congressman Henry Reuss reads, "The Congress may enact laws regulating the amounts of contributions and expenditures intended to affect congressional elections."[13] Yet the likelihood of an overturning of some or all of *Buckley*, either by the Court or by amendment, does not appear to be very great. The Constitution of the United States remains therefore the greatest single limitation to legislated change in campaign finance.

Second, there are substantial political limits to any reform of the PACs. They do not, however, center in the American electorate. Mass opinion appears to be consistently in favor of reform, as it is also on questions of limiting campaign contributions. As recently as 1978, for example, the Louis Harris poll showed an almost 2–1 ratio in favor of cutting in half the ceiling on PAC contributions to individual candidates.[14]

The political climate within Congress and the parties is far more variable. Concern runs highest about the independent expenditures and "negative" campaigns of the unaffiliated PACs of the right. Their campaigns most profoundly threaten the members of Congress and the status quo in campaigning generally; the independent campaign is probably the only true innovation that the PACs have brought to American politics. Moreover, of all the PACs, they most frequently campaign against the incumbent members of Congress. Finally, they have no affiliated organizations with political influence or a network of legislative relationships to protect them.

The members of Congress are of a mixed mind, however, about the affiliated PACs and their more conventional giving to congressional candidates. Just one table from a survey of 1978 candidates for the House commissioned by a House committee (Table 8–1) sketches the outlines of the disagreement. Conservatives, incumbents, and Republicans are clearly more favorably disposed to PACs than liberals, challengers, and Democrats. In addition, the author of the study, Gary Orren, reports that "the more PAC funds a campaign received, the more it welcomed their growing influence," although a "substantial number" of PAC-supported candidates expressed "grave doubts"

Table 8-1
**Attitudes Toward Political Action Committees,
1978 House General Election Candidates***

	Desirable, %	Neutral, %	Undesirable, %
Democrats			
Liberal Democrats	26	14	60
Moderate Democrats	31	20	49
Conservative Democrats	47	20	33
Republicans			
Liberal Republicans	17	33	50
Moderate Republicans	47	23	30
Conservative Republicans	53	27	20
Liberals			
Incumbents	41	21	38
Nonincumbents	0	8	92
Moderates			
Incumbents	42	21	37
Nonincumbents	30	21	49
Conservatives			
Incumbents	57	22	21
Nonincumbents	49	26	25
Liberals	25	16	59
Moderates	37	21	42
Conservatives	50	25	25

Source: Kennedy Institute Study for Committee on House Administration, cited in note 15.

*Responses to the question: "Do you feel that the increasing importance of PACs is desirable or undesirable?"

about their power.[15] The 1979 vote on the Obey-Railsback proposal to limit PAC spending leads to the same conclusion: Democrats and liberals voted heavily for it; conservatives and Republicans voted overwhelmingly against it.[16]

But how quickly the reform coalitions "reform"! In 1974, in the Senate, it was Republican Howard Baker who proposed that political groups and committees be prohibited from making political contributions:

> I do not think purely political action groups should be permitted to contribute. They cannot vote. . . . So, why should they be allowed to contribute?[17]

And, in the 1976 aftermath of *Buckley v. Valeo*, a coalition mostly of Republicans and Southern Democrats supported another Senate attempt (which narrowly failed) to ban the contributions of nonparty committees.[18] But those were days of ascendancy for the labor PACs. As PAC fortunes and their patterns of growth and contribution turn, so obviously—and very quickly—do attitudes about them.

Third, reform depends on the government's ability to carry it out or to administer it effectively. The elements of speed and fairness are critical (if for no other reason than that there is a campaign going on) whether one talks of disclosure of new financial information or monitoring of political activities not monitored previously. We must thus confront the record and condition of the FEC, Congress's chosen instrument for administering legislation on campaign finance, and examine its capacity for new administrative burdens.[19]

Virtually all observers give high marks to the FEC's services to the press, scholars, and the inquiring public. Those clienteles sometimes wish that the FEC collected and reported its data in different ways, but that kind of complaint probably can never be stilled. Moreover, the FEC has achieved a high level of compliance and reporting by candidates and committees. While it obviously cannot claim all the credit for the successful reporting, it certainly can take some.

Yet the FEC has had and continues to have serious problems. The commission itself has repeatedly divided along party lines, and it has suffered also from a lack of continuity in leadership. The effects of those problems have been compounded by internal jockeying for authority on the staff of the commission. Above all, though, the commission and the staff suffer from being kept on a very short and tight congressional leash. Individual members of Congress have heaped abuse on the FEC, and late appropriations and threats of budget cuts leave the staff in a state of chronic insecurity. Until the Supreme Court ruled the legislative veto unconstitutional in mid-1983, Congress held a veto over the commission's rules and regulations. Moreover, Congress does not permit the random auditing of candidates' reports. At the same time, the FEC hears criticism of alleged "nitpicking" in its rules and audits and of what candidates think is its failure to recognize the realities of contemporary campaigning.

Regardless of the causes of the FEC's condition, it does not appear to have administrative capacity "in reserve" for new tasks. Indeed, it may now be strained to the very limit; the final reports on the 1979–80 election cycle, for instance, did not appear until early 1982. (The commission's staff for dealing with the 1982 campaign is smaller than it was five years ago.) Nor does there seem to be much desire in Congress to strengthen or even stabilize the FEC. Although an attempt to cripple or abolish it was easily beaten back in 1981, few voices were raised in its praise. The early 1980s are a time of deregulation rather than strengthened regulation in all industries and enterprises. Furthermore, it is clear that many members of Congress have little affection for the status quo after less than ten years of complying with their own legislation. It is the usual reaction of a regulated industry toward governmental regulation. In this case, however, the "regulated industry" also approves the regulations and funds of the regulator.

The Obey-Railsback Proposal

After passing the 1976 amendments to the FECA, Congress wrestled seriously with reform of PACs only once—in the Obey-Railsback proposal of 1979.[20] It might be argued that the attempts to expend public financing to congressional elections were in a sense an attempt to reform the PACs, but public financing has far broader goals than just the PACs.

The Obey-Railsback proposal contained two chief components. The first would have cut in half the limit on PAC spending in a campaign from $5,000 to $2,500. (By the time final passage was voted in the House, the limit was raised to $3,000.) The second component would have set a new aggregate limit of $50,000 in PAC contributions to any congressional candidate. That is, no candidate could receive more than $50,000 from PACs in a two-year election cycle. (On the floor of the House the limit was eventually raised to $70,000.) Those provisions, and several others, were to apply only to candidates for the House of Representatives. Eventually the Obey-Railsback proposal passed the House by a vote of 217–198. Organized labor supported it, perhaps out of a sense of foreboding about the growth of PACs, and support for it on the floor came primarily from liberals and Democrats. Democrats were 188 to 74 in favor; Republicans were 124 to 29 in opposition. The

Senate, under threat of a Republican filibuster, never considered the bill.

The two restrictions of Obey-Railsback would have affected the PACs differently. A relatively small number of PAC contributions to House candidates in 1978 exceeded the proposed $6,000 ceiling ($3,000 for the primary and $3,000 for the general election).[21] But the aggregate limits would probably have affected the candidates more drastically. Richard Conlon of the Democratic Study Group calculated that 176 House candidates in 1977–78 exceeded the $50,000 figure in receipts from PACs.[22] The future effects of an Obey-Railsback provision would be more difficult to predict. Many observers, including the PACs themselves, think it would push PACs into more independent campaigns.[23] Possibly, though, while some PACs would venture more deeply into independent expenditures, others might respond by spreading their contributions more widely. There might then be an increase of PAC contributions to the less senior, less powerful members of Congress.

The pros and cons of the Obey-Railsback debate are now its major legacy to the reform question. The case for the legislation rested chiefly on concern both about the ability of large PAC contributors to reach and use centers of influence in the legislative process and about the general growth of PACs and PAC giving, especially among the corporate and conservative PACs. The case against it was more diffuse. In part it was a defense of the growth of PACs sympathetic to conservative and Republican candidates; in part it reflected a conviction about the futility of legislated change and the danger of unloosing more unanticipated consequences for American campaign finance; and in part it grew from a fear that curtailing the money supply would make it harder for challengers to mount successful campaigns against entrenched incumbents. Behind the debate was the issue that was in everyone's mind as Congress legislated on PACs throughout the 1970s: the balance of political influence between labor and business. Opponents of Obey-Railsback assumed that corporations and business associations would lose some of the effectiveness of their new political weapon, while labor's non-PAC activities would go on without restriction.

Option One: Public Finance

Neither legislative logic nor political reality permits us to separate the issue of PACs from the wider questions about the funding of American campaigns. The first policy issue about the PACs, therefore, is the choice between private and public funding. If we reject public funding—that is, the partial or total funding of campaigns by taxpayers via the treasury of the United States—we then proceed to assemble the best (or the least objectionable) system of voluntary, private funding. But the public-private funding issue is paramount.

Most of the critics of PAC contributions and activities are critics of other aspects of the status quo in campaign finance. For many of them, the reform solution of choice is public financing of congressional elections. After what appeared to be the successful inauguration of public financing of presidential elections in 1976—the acceptance of it both by the public and the Supreme Court[24]—President Carter and a number of prominent Democrats in Congress supported proposals in the late 1970s for its extension to congressional races. A certain desperation marked their efforts. In the words of former Congressman Abner Mikva:

> As the special interest Political Action Committees become more entrenched, they will become an insurmountable lobby against campaign finance reform. The PACs already have a lot invested. . . . So this year may be the last best hope for public financing—and the last best hope for a more open and less tainted election process.[25]

The Senate voted for public funding in both 1973 and 1974. No proposal for public funding, however, has ever passed the House. While the fear of PAC power among the liberals and Democrats in the House was rising, it was not enough to offset the loss of steam in the reform movement as memories of Watergate grew dimmer.

"Public funding" proposals differ in important details, and yet they tend to have a good deal in common. Recent proposals have generally provided for limited public funding, usually based on the candidate's ability to raise matching funds from private contributors, a system already in effect for the preconvention phases of presidential campaigns. The proposals have also had spending limits—such as $150,000 for a House campaign—with the provision in some that the ceiling would be waived or raised if one candidate refused to accept public funding. (The purpose clearly is to encourage that acceptance by reducing the advantage of not doing so.) Most provided for financing from a fund created by checkoffs on income tax returns, again drawing on the precedents of presidential campaign funding. In 1978, the Democratic authors of one bill also included a section limiting contributions to congressional campaigns by party committees. In view of the recent success of Republican party fundraising, the provision struck many observers as more than usually partisan and contributed to the solid Republican opposition to the bill (140–0) and its defeat by a 198–209 vote in the House.[26]

The plans for public funding, of course, assume that large numbers of candidates will accept it and, as a condition of doing so, will accept limits on contributions and expenditures. (On this point it is well to keep in mind that some candidates have renounced public funding in the states, and that in 1980 John Connally, a contender for the Republican presidential nomination, did not accept it.)[27] Anything less than public funding, its supporters believe, will only patch up a few of the worst spots in a fatally infirm system of private campaign finance. And it remains the only way left after *Buckley* to equalize ("democratize") the resources for political influence, whether that equalization is between incumbents and challengers, rich and poor candidates, or Democrats and Republicans.

Even the vocabulary changes when we turn to the opposition to public funding. The option becomes "taxpayer financing" of campaigns, and the proposals come to be known as "incumbent protection" or "incumbent welfare" bills. Opponents have almost universally accepted the conclusion of political scientist Gary Jacobson that any limit or restriction on funds for campaigning for Congress will work to the advantage of incumbents and to the disadvantage of challengers because challengers must spend larger sums to overcome the political advantages of incumbency.[28] Many Republicans and conservatives also resist public funding on more general ideological grounds: a distrust of government regulation generally and a distaste for taking money from taxpayers for candidates and causes they might not approve of. Indeed, it is that broad ideological opposition, combined with an awareness of the very healthy condition of Republican party fundraising, that will very likely keep Republican incumbents from supporting public funding. In addition, the sources of labor's political power—its activities, its communications, and its registration and get-out-the-vote campaigns—would continue under public funding.[29] It thus would appear that public funding is a program of Democratic majorities in Congress.

Finally, in the past ten years or so, a number of proposals have been advanced that involved in-kind public funding: free television time, for example, or grants of printing or free postage, or publicly prepared campaign brochures for all candidates. Perhaps the most radical proposal of them all is the one for a "voucher" system in which voters would receive coupons (redeemable in cash or campaign goods), which they would be free to give to the candidates, parties, or PACs of their choice.[30]

Option Two: Private Finance

If public financing is rejected, reform must affect the present mix of private funding sources. The first and most obvious strategy is to place some kind of limit on the flow of private money. But the Supreme Court's interpretation of the First Amendment precludes limits on candidates' expenditures, independent expenditures, and candidates' use of their own resources. It should also be remembered that the present limits on individual and PAC contributions were adopted in 1974 and that, in the absence of congressional adjustment, inflation, the great regulator, has effectively cut them in half. Nevertheless, further restrictions on contributions to candidates are possible—there are repeated proposals to cut the PAC ceiling below its present $5,000 per candidate per election—but there remains considerable uncertainty over the extent of the limits the Court will tolerate. Like the Obey-Railsback proposal, a more recent one in a comprehensive bill by Congressmen Obey, Leach, and Glickman (Democrat of Wisconsin, Republican of Iowa, and Democrat of Kansas) defines a new kind of limit: one on the aggregate receipts from one kind of contributor. Specifically, the proposed limit would be on the amounts candidates could accept from PACs collectively; by the 1982 proposal this limit had risen to $90,000.[31] The Supreme Court has never considered the constitutionality of such a limit.

The alternative strategy is to encourage an increase in other sources of private funding: the parties or individual contributors. (There are only four sources of private campaign funds: parties, individuals, PACs, and the personal wealth of the candidates themselves.) This strategy of countervailing power seeks to reduce the importance of the PACs by encouraging their competitors. Various proposals would double the present limit of $1,000 on individual contributions or would raise the limit on party contributions from $10,000 to $30,000. Some commentators also hope to encourage individual contributors by raising the tax credit to 100 percent or by raising the statutory limits on individual contributions.[32] Others have proposed bolstering the party role in campaign finance—which may already be happening because of the parties' own initiatives. Richard Richards, former chair of the Republican National Committee, proposed in late 1981 the removal of all limits on party contributions. Others have urged less drastic moves in the same direction.

Regulating the financing of campaigns by imposing limits on contributions is a bit like grabbing a half-inflated balloon. One squeezes it, even contains it, at one point, only to have it expand at another. If direct PAC contributions are limited, independent expenditures may increase. Limiting big contributors forces candidates and PACs to raise money in small sums and thus inflates the importance of emotional mail appeals and the mailing-list entrepreneurs. And if we limit voluntary sources, we open the way for the recruitment of more and more candidates of considerable personal wealth. In short, the search for limited reform of the private system—especially when the Supreme Court will permit no limits on expenditures—is at best an exercise in complicated projections, obscure trade-offs, and Hobson's choices, leading to nagging fears about the prospect of even more unanticipated consequences.

The Problem of Independent Campaigns

One policy issue remains apart from the public-private funding choices: the rise of independent expenditures and the often "negative" independent campaign. Even the most massive program of public funding would have no effect per se on them—except perhaps to increase them. The ability of Congress to limit independent expenditures even as a necessary auxiliary to a program of public funding is not clear. In 1981 the Supreme Court, divided 4-4, upheld a lower court decision that invalidated the FECA limitation on independent expenditures in presidential election campaigns if the major party candidates accepted public funding and thus the limits on expenditures.[33] That specific issue, and the more general one of the power of Congress to limit independent expenditures, has returned to the federal courts in mid-1983.

Less draconian measures do not readily leap to mind. The major policy suggestion so far seems to have originated with Common Cause's Fred Wertheimer. Writing in the *New York Times,* he proposed giving equal time on radio or television to candidates attacked by an independent campaigner. It is not clear who would pay for the equal time, but if it were the media station or stations, the effect would clearly be to close down access to the media in the first place. Since PACs could present their views of issues, parties, or candidates without attacking other candidates, and thus without triggering the equal-time rule, "positive" independent campaigns might be encouraged. However, fearful and vulnerable station owners might well be unwilling to take that chance.[34]

* * *

There is a realistic pessimism among the reformers about the political climate for reform in 1983 and 1984. Watergate recedes from memory a little bit more each year, and confidence in governmental regulation of any activity is at a low point for this generation. The Supreme Court has raised constitutional barriers to regulation and left the authority of Congress unclear. A government divided between Democrats and Republicans adds one more difficulty. And the unanticipated consequences of the reforms of the 1970s only underscore the problems and uncertainties of legislating on campaign finance. Holes are plugged only to create pressure for new ones; constitutionally protected activity appears unexpectedly; and legislators seem unable to predict the effects of their actions.

It is discouraging, too, not to be able to easily define a policy problem to address. At times it seems that there is an almost infinite sequence of reform issues. We cannot deal with PACs unless we deal with all of campaign finance, and we cannot deal with campaign finance unless we confront the state of the parties and the rest of our electoral institutions. Therefore, it is perhaps most useful to focus on political organizations and their important mission in organizing and aggregating individuals in the political system. Can the parties be rehabilitated sufficiently for them to retake some of the political territory they lost over the last generation or two? If not, what alternatives are there to the parties? Are there, indeed, any other options—or any other acceptable options—than the interest groups and their offspring, the PACs? Ultimately, reform of campaign finance involves a decision about the kind of political organizations—political intermediaries and brokers—we want for American electoral politics.

NOTES

Chapter 1

1. The figures on the number of PACs come from the reports of the FEC. The number, it should be noted, is the total number of PACs registered with the FEC. In any election, the number actually active is somewhat less; in 1982, for example, it was 2,651.
2. 2 U.S.C. sec. 431(4).
3. 26 U.S.C. sec. 9001(9).
4. 2 U.S.C. sec. 441a(a).
5. Ibid.
6. 2 U.S.C. sec. 441b(b).
7. Ibid.
8. For excellent surveys of the rise of PACs over the past several decades, see the two reports of Joseph E. Cantor for the Congressional Research Service of the Library of Congress: *Political Action Committees: Their Evolution and Growth and Their Implication for the Political System*, rev. ed. (Washington, D.C.: CRS, 1982), identified as CRS Report 82–92 GOV; and *The Evolution of Issues Surrounding Independent Expenditures in Election Campaigns* (Washington, D.C.: CRS, 1982), identified as CRS Report 82–87 GOV.

Chapter 2

1. Edwin M. Epstein, "Business and Labor under the Federal Election Campaign Act of 1971," in *Parties, Interest Groups, and Campaign Finance Laws*, ed. Michael J. Malbin (Washington, D.C.: American Enterprise Institute, 1980), p. 110. On the origins of PACs, see also Herbert E. Alexander, *Financing Politics: Money, Election and Political Reform* (Washington, D.C.: Congressional Quarterly, 1976), and *Financing the 1976 Election* (Washington, D.C.: Congressional Quarterly, 1979), pp. 559–66.
2. Bernadette A. Budde, "Business Political Action Committees," in

Parties, Interest Groups, and Campaign Finance Laws, ed. Malbin, p. 10.

3. Epstein, "Business and Labor under the Federal Election Campaign Act," pp. 109, 145.

4. For a history of PAC response to the legislation, see Epstein, "Business and Labor under the Federal Election Campaign Act," and Xandra Kayden, "The Impact of the FECA on the Growth and Evolution of Political Action Committees," sec. 5 of *An Analysis of the Impact of the Federal Election Campaign Act, 1972–78*, report by the Campaign Finance Study Group at the Kennedy School, Harvard University, to the House Committee on House Administration (May 1979). On separate segregated funds, 2 U.S.C. sec. 441b.

5. 2 U.S.C. sec. 434.

6. 2 U.S.C. sec 441a(a).

7. 2 U.S.C. sec. 441c.

8. The creation and regulation of the public financing of presidential elections can be found at 26 U.S.C. sec. 9001–9042.

9. The commission divided 4–2 in the SunPac advisory opinion; see FEC Advisory Opinion 1975–23 (December 3, 1975).

10. *Buckley v. Valeo*, 424 U.S. 1 (1976).

11. The issue of the constitutionality of limits on independent expenditures in publicly funded elections has been reopened in 1983 and will be treated in later chapters of this paper.

12. This summary, of course, simplifies and omits some details of regulation; they are all contained in 2 U.S.C. sec. 431–55. For concise, how-to-do-it advice on these matters, see Curtis Sproul, "A Primer for Corporate and Union Political Action Committees," *The Practical Lawyer* 24 (July 15, September 1, 1978): 29–50, 61–72; and Sproul, "Corporations and Unions in Federal Politics: A Practical Approach to Federal Election Law Compliance," *Arizona Law Review* 22 (1980): 465–518.

13. It is perhaps pertinent also to note that contributions to PACs enjoy the same deductibility under the Internal Revenue Code as do contributions to candidates, with two caveats, however. First, the PAC must be contributing primarily to candidates; contributions to PACs whose primary purpose is lobbying or political education, for example, do not qualify. Second, the deductibility of contributions to PACs spending most of their funds in independent campaigns or expenditures—PACs, in other words, that do not make contributions to candidates—is under challenge before the Internal Revenue Service.

14. A third set of data on the number of PACs has appeared from time to time in FEC reports. It is a cumulative total of all PACs ever registered with the FEC (rather than a total of those in existence at any one time). In late 1982, that cumulative total was 3,727.

15. Note that Table 2–3 deals only with general election candidates,

while Table 2–2 includes all candidates; that is to say, Table 2–3 does not include candidates who lost in the primary. The more limited set of data in Table 2–3 is more appropriate for year-to-year comparisons because the number of candidates in general elections is a more nearly constant number than the total of all candidates. FEC data for 1980 on the relative importance of the various kinds of contributors to congressional campaigns indicate that 26 percent of all of the receipts of general election candidates for Congress came from PACs. Another 3 percent came from the parties. (That figure does not include party expenditures on behalf of the candidates.) Of the remaining 71 percent contributed by individuals, probably some 10 to 12 percent came from the resources of the candidates themselves and their families. Preliminary estimates for 1982 indicate a similar pattern.

16. The Wisconsin data are reported by David Adamany, "PAC's and the Democratic Financing of Politics," *Arizona Law Review* 22 (1980): 588.

17. The California data are reported in Epstein, "The PAC Phenomenon: An Overview," *Arizona Law Review* 22 (1980): 362. Epstein specifically notes that his data carry only part of the way through the 1980 campaign and thus underestimate PAC growth in California.

18. Data from the reports of the Minnesota Ethical Practices Board. It should be noted that the prohibition against corporate PACs is being challenged at the moment in federal district court in Minnesota in light of the Supreme Court's decisions in *Buckley v. Valeo*, 424 U.S. 1 (1976), and *First National Bank of Boston v. Bellotti*, 435 U.S. 765 (1978).

19. For the publications, see *Campaign Practices Reports* (Washington, D.C.: Congressional Quarterly, biweekly), *PACs and Lobbies* (Washington, D.C.: Zuckerman, semimonthly), *Campaigns and Elections* (Washington, D.C.: Reed, quarterly), and Commerce Clearing House, *Federal Election Campaign Finance Reporter*.

20. Lee Ann Elliott, "Political Action Committees—Precincts of the 80's," *Arizona Law Review* 22 (1980): 540.

Chapter 3

1. See also Michael J. Malbin, "Of Mountains and Molehills: PACs, Campaigns, and Public Policy," *Parties, Interest Groups, and Campaign Finance Laws* (Washington, D.C.: American Enterprise Institute, 1980), pp. 164–65, on the percentage of candidate receipts given by PACs and more generally on PAC support for incumbents.

2. It may be that the lower level of support for Senate chairs reflects the lesser influence of the committee system in the Senate. Data are not yet available for a parallel analysis for 1982.

3. Two related points should be noted on the incumbency factor.

First, incumbent strategy may change in midcampaign; contributors may begin by supporting incumbents and then shift to challengers as the campaigns develop and their outcomes seem clearer. Second, some substantial part of the aid to incumbents is given in the nonelection years, the years in which members of Congress customarily hold their fundraising dinners to which lobbyists, Washington representatives, and PAC managers are "invited."

4. On the timing of contributions and the value of seed money, see Michael Malbin, statement at Round Table on Political Action Committees, Citizens' Research Foundation Conference on the FECA (Washington, D.C.: April 3, 1981). It is excerpted in Herbert E. Alexander and Brian A. Haggerty, *The Federal Election Campaign Act: After a Decade of Political Reform* (Los Angeles: Citizens' Research Foundation, 1981).

5. William Kroger, "Business PACs Are Coming of Age," *Nation's Business* (October 1978), p. 41.

6. *Buckley v. Valeo*, 424 U.S. 1 (1976); the Court upholds independent expenditures at pp. 39–51.

7. 2 U.S.C. sec. 431(17).

8. Herbert Alexander, *Financing the 1976 Election* (Washington, D.C.: Congressional Quarterly, 1979), pp. 521–22.

9. The largest individual independent expenditure was that of Cecil Hayden, a Texas industrialist, at $600,000. Stewart Mott was second, at $110,000.

10. Not all independent expenditures employ the media, though. The League of Conservation Voters, for one, spent "much" of its $500,000 reported in 1980 in an independent campaign of door-to-door canvassing by young volunteers and workers in selected congressional races. *Congressional Quarterly* (January 31, 1981), p. 213.

11. *Common Cause v. Schmitt*, 102 S.Ct. 1266 (1982). The statutory section in question is at 26 U.S.C. sec. 9012(f).

12. See Advisory Opinion 1983–10 of the Federal Election Commission, issued on May 18, 1983.

Chapter 4

1. Here and generally on Senator Helms, see Elizabeth Drew, "A Reporter at Large (Jesse Helms)," *The New Yorker*, July 20, 1982, pp. 78–95; and "Sen. Helms Builds a Machine of Interlinked Organizations to Shape Both Politics, Policy," *Congressional Quarterly Weekly Report* (March 6, 1982), pp. 499–505.

2. Drew, "Reporter at Large," p. 81.

3. "Spending smarter on political candidates," *Business Week*, November 3, 1980, p. 42.

4. Steven Roberts, "Helping PACs Decide How to Spend Their Money," *New York Times*, September 10, 1982.

5. These five accounted for 42 percent of the grand total of $1.8 million. No other PAC received as much as $50,000 from other PACs. As usual, data come from the reports of the FEC.

6. Maxwell Glen, "The PACs Are Back, Richer and Wiser, to Finance the 1980 Elections," *National Journal*, November 24, 1979, p. 1982.

7. Richard Cohen, "Congressional Democrats Beware—Here Come the Corporate PACs," *National Journal*, August 8, 1980, p. 1305.

8. Commentary in Malbin, *Parties, Interest Groups, and Campaign Finance Laws* (Washington, D.C.: American Enterprise Institute, 1980), p. 196.

9. Common Cause, *Money, Power, and Politics in the 97th Congress*, p. i.

10. Albert R. Hunt, "Special-Interest Money Increasingly Influences What Congress Enacts," *Wall Street Journal*, July 26, 1982. More generally on the legislative connection, see Elizabeth Drew's two-part series in *The New Yorker* on "Politics and Money," December 6, 13, 1982.

11. 2 U.S.C. sec. 431(9)(B)(ii, iii).

12. Michael Malbin, "Labor, Business, and Money—A Post-Election Analysis," *National Journal*, March 19, 1977, pp. 412–17.

13. Herbert E. Alexander, *Financing the 1980 Election* (Boston: D.C. Heath, 1983).

14. Edwin M. Epstein, "Business and Labor under the Federal Election Campaign Act of 1971," in *Parties, Interest Groups, and Campaign Finance Laws*, ed. Malbin, p. 146.

Chapter 5

1. *Encyclopedia of Associations* (Detroit: Gale, 1980), reported in *Statistical Abstract of the United States* (Washington, D.C.: U.S. Government Printing Office, 1980), p. 57.

2. Bernadette A. Budde, "The Practical Role of Corporate PAC's in the Political Process," *Arizona Law Review* 22 (1980): 561.

3. It is interesting and useful to speculate about why we know more about corporate PACs than, say, labor PACs. The corporate PACs are more widely reported, both because of the greater number of their publications and because of their greater willingness and desire to spread their message. Labor, on the other hand, is less open and less confident about candid discussion of its political activities. It has neither the network of publications nor the professional infrastructure that corporate PACs do. It is also clear that labor lacks the missionary incentive

for spreading the word about the PAC movement that corporations have.

4. Edwin M. Epstein, "Business and Labor under the Federal Election Campaign Act of 1971," in *Parties, Interest Groups, and Campaign Finance Laws*, ed. Michael J. Malbin (Washington, D.C.: American Enterprise Institute,1980), p. 127. The overall percentage for the top 1,000 and the leading 300 nonindustrial corporations is 28 percent.

5. Budde, director of political education for BIPAC, quoted in Vernon Louviere, "Every Candidate Needs a Landslide of Dollars," *Nation's Business* (October 1979), p. 44.

6. For a comparable listing of reasons, see Edward Handler and John R. Mulkern, *Business in Politics* (Lexington, Mass.: Lexington Books, 1982), p. 61:

> PAC officers were asked to indicate what, in their view, was the dominant consideration influencing their corporation's decision to sponsor a PAC. The five motivations most frequently mentioned by respondents (in order of priority) are (1) management recognition of the significant impact of government on corporate operations; (2) acknowledgment of the need of the corporation's Washington representative for adequate income with which to respond to the escalating importunities of congressmen and senators; (3) enhancement of political participation opportunities for managerial employees as part of their civic responsibility; (4) pressures felt by CEOs to emulate the example of peers who are reporting a successful experience with PACs; and (5) development of an effective counterbalance to the political influence of adversary organizations, particularly unions.

7. Quoted in Morton Mintz, *Washington Post*, September 25, 1980, p. A2. It may also be relevant that Mr. Shapiro was identified in the 1970s as a leading Democrat among the presidents and chairmen of America's large corporations.

8. For interesting examples, see reports in the *New York Times* of Robert Samuels's role in founding Senior PAC (March 1, 1982) and Victor Kamber's in the creation of Progressive PAC (February 10, 1982).

9. The NABPAC questionnaire of late 1980 puts the figure at 20 percent; a multigroup questionnaire of November 1981 put it at 18 percent. (The latter survey enjoyed the sponsorship of Business-Industry PAC, NABPAC, the National Association of Manufacturers, and the Public Affairs Council.) Handler and Mulkern also arrive at a 20 percent figure.

10. The right of Sun Oil to solicit its workers was, of course, an issue in its request for an advisory opinion from the FEC in 1975. Following the FEC's favorable opinion, though, Congress made "crossover" sol-

icitations more difficult and less attractive in its 1976 amendments to the FECA.

11. Many PACs that make earmarking available do not encourage it, and only a small percentage of contributors to them take advantage of it. Earmarking, therefore, accounts for a much smaller percentage of total PAC receipts than the percentage of PACs making it available might suggest.

12. Not surprisingly, some PAC managers whose careful solicitations produce contribution rates well below 30 percent think that figures in the 80 percent or above range are the result of excessively vigorous and zealous solicitations. They recognize, however, that there are different corporate subcultures and that some will produce more uniform, conforming behavior than others.

13. The first estimate comes from a 1978 survey of corporate PACs by the Public Affairs Council; the second is from the National Association of Business PAC's (NABPAC) survey of December 1980 almost two years later; the third is from the multigroup study of November 1981.

14. Herbert E. Alexander, *Financing the 1976 Election* (Boston: D.C. Heath, 1983), pp. 824–25.

15. See the multigroup study of November 1981.

16. Of the charges of coercion, the best known was that made by the International Association of Machinists. The IAM sought unsuccessfully to get the FEC to investigate the contributions to the ten largest corporate PACs for signs of coercion. When the FEC dismissed the IAM request, the IAM challenged that dismissal in the U.S. District Court for the District of Columbia. Again the IAM suit was dismissed.

17. See Curtis C. Sproul, "A Primer for Corporate and Union Political Action Committees," *The Practical Lawyer* 24 (July 15, 1978): 47.

18. Maxwell Glen, "The PACs Are Back, Richer and Wiser, To Finance the 1980 Elections," *National Journal*, November 24, 1979, p. 1982.

19. *Congressional Quarterly*, October 25, 1980, p. 3204.

20. For a look into the decision-making process in one, that of Sun Oil, see Robert Hershey's report of his observation of the SunPAC's contribution committee in the throes of decision in the *New York Times*, October 13, 1982. For more systematic data on decision-making, see Handler and Mulkern, *Business in Politics*, pp. 66–96.

21. The concept of "exit" is perceptively analyzed in Albert O. Hirschman, *Exit, Voice, and Loyalty* (Cambridge, Mass.: Harvard University Press, 1970).

Chapter 6

1. On the decline of the parties, see David Broder, *The Party's Over* (New York: Harper and Row, 1971), and Walter Dean Burnham, *Critical Elections and the Mainsprings of American Politics* (New York: Norton, 1970).

2. On the new activism, see Sidney Verba and Norman Nie, *Participation in America* (New York: Harper and Row, 1972).

3. For 1979–80, the National Rifle Association reported $804,000 in communication costs to the FEC, a figure that placed it at the top of the list. It was followed in size of communication expenditures by four labor unions.

4. Maxwell Glen, "The PACs Are Back, Richer and Wiser, To Finance the 1980 Elections," *National Journal,* November 24, 1979, p. 1982.

5. On nominations as the critical and central business of political parties, see V. O. Key, Jr., *American State Politics* (New York: Knopf, 1956), chap. 6.

6. See William Poe, "Pac-to-Pac Radio Ads," *Washington Journalism Review* (September 1981).

7. Debate on Obey-Railsback proposal to reduce limits on PAC spending, *Congressional Record* 125 (October 17, 1979), p. H9291.

8. The eligible electorate is composed of all Americans eligible to register and vote. It is a somewhat smaller group than the total of all Americans aged eighteen and older; aliens, for example, must be excluded from that total.

9. The CPS's survey in 1980 also asked its respondents which political action groups they gave to, but one has to keep in mind the initial question of PACs to evaluate the responses to that question. The first question asked:

> Now, what about political action groups such as groups sponsored by a union or business, or issue groups like the National Rifle Association or the National Organization for Women? Did you give money this election year to a political action group or any other group that supported or opposed particular candidates in this election?

The largest number of specific responses to the follow-up question ("Which political action groups did you give to?") mentioned labor unions. But the second- and third-largest totals were achieved by the two groups specifically mentioned in the primary question: NOW and pro-ERA groups and antigun control groups. The power of suggestion would appear to have been revalidated. In fact, the inability of the respondents to mention a very wide or very representative group of

PACs casts some doubt on the validity of some responses to the initial question, too.

10. That figure is consistent with PAC receipt totals reported in some states. Moreover, the total of $260 million is a credible figure in relation to the $1.2 billion total cost of all national, state, and local campaigns in 1980.

11. Michael J. Malbin, "Of Mountains and Molehills: PACs, Campaigns, and Public Policy," *Parties, Interest Groups, and Campaign Finance Laws* (Washington, D.C.: American Enterprise Institute, 1980), p. 152.

12. U.S. Congress, House Committee on House Administration, "Public Financing of Congressional Elections," Hearings, 96th Cong., 1st sess., March 15–27, 1979, p. 338.

Chapter 7

1. Americans are often surprised, moreover, to discover that, when one standardizes for cost of living, other countries spend a good deal more per voter than we do. See, for example, the symposium in the *Journal of Politics* 25 (August 1963).

2. Data from U.S. Bureau of the Census, *Statistical Abstract of the United States: 1981* (Washington, D.C.: U.S. Government Printing Office, 1981).

3. Walter K. Moore, "The Case of an Independent Political Action Committee," in *Parties, Interest Groups, and Campaign Finance Laws*, ed. Michael J. Malbin (Washington, D.C.: American Enterprise Institute, 1980), p. 65.

4. *Los Angeles Times*, October 12, 1982.

5. For a useful statement of the problem and the scholarly literature, see Virginia Held, *The Public Interest and Individual Interests* (New York: Basic Books, 1970).

6. U.S. Congress, House Committee on House Administration, "Public Financing of Congressional Election," Hearings, 96th Cong., 1st sess., March 15–27, 1979, p. 295.

7. See, for example, Albert R. Hunt in the *Wall Street Journal*, July 26, 1982.

8. Again, even though her articles deal broadly with political finance, Elizabeth Drew returns repeatedly to the issue of legislative influence in her two-part series on "Politics and Money" in *The New Yorker*, December 6, 13, 1982.

9. *Washington Post*, November 9, 1982.

10. For reports that many members of Congress think the connection between money and legislative voting is greatly exaggerated, see Richard E. Cohen, "Giving Till It Hurts: 1982 Campaign Prompts

New Look at Financing Races," *National Journal*, December 18, 1982, pp. 2144–53.

11. On the power of incumbents, see Morris Fiorina, *Congress: Keystone of the Washington Establishment* (New Haven: Yale University Press, 1977).

12. Gary Jacobson, *Money in Congressional Elections* (New Haven: Yale University Press, 1980).

13. Cadell's report appeared on the Op-Ed page of the *New York Times*, November 14, 1982. The *Times* study, reported by Adam Clymer, appeared in that paper on November 5, 1982.

14. For the end of the debate between the *Washington Post* and Terry Dolan, of the NCPAC, see Dolan's rebuttal to news coverage on November 7, 1982, and then David Broder's surrebuttal on November 10, 1982. The one NCPAC "victory" that all agree on was the defeat of Senator Howard Cannon of Nevada.

15. David Jessup, "Can Political Influence Be Democratized? A Labor Perspective," in *Parties, Interest Groups, and Campaign Finance Laws*, ed. Malbin, p. 26. (Emphasis removed.)

16. *Buckley v. Valeo*, 424 U.S. 1 (1976), pp. 48–49.

17. Debate on the Obey-Railsback proposal to reduce PAC spending limits, *Congressional Record* 125 (October 17, 1979), p. H9281.

18. Once again, the reporting on NCPAC provides an example. In 1981, Terry Dolan wrote members of Congress that "a number of our contributors" felt strongly about a tax shelter (commodity straddles) known largely to traders in the commodity markets. The major contributor in question turned out to be a member of the Chicago Board of Trade who was both a heavy contributor to NCPAC and a member of its executive committee. See Bill Keller, "Commodity Straddles New Dogma at NCPAC," *Congressional Quarterly*, July 4, 1981, p. 1191.

Chapter 8

1. That was essentially the position of the plaintiffs in *Buckley v. Valeo*. For a longer development of their position, see Brice M. Clagett and John R. Bolton, "*Buckley v. Valeo*, Its Aftermath and Its Prospects: The Constitutionality of Government Restraints on Political Campaign Financing," *Vanderbilt Law Review* 29 (November 1976): 1327–83.

2. *Buckley v. Valeo*, 424 U.S. 1 (1976).

3. Ibid., pp. 20–21.

4. Ibid., p. 45.

5. Ibid.

6. Ibid., pp. 48–49.

7. Ibid., p. 57.

8. Justice Stevens took no part in the case; Justice Stewart, the only departee from the Court since the decision, voted with the majority on all questions.

9. 435 U.S. 765 (1978).

10. Ibid., pp. 784–85.

11. *Citizens Against Rent Control v. City of Berkeley*, 102 S.Ct. 434 1981).

12. J. Skelly Wright, "Big Bucks in Politics: Sin Against the Constitution," *Washington Post*, October 31, 1982. See also his article in the *Columbia Law Review* 82 (May 1982): 609–45.

13. *Congressional Record*, June 23, 1982, p. H3901.

14. *Chicago Tribune*, May 29, 1978, sec. 2, p. 3.

15. Gary R. Orren, "The Impact of the Federal Election Campaign Act: The View from the Campaigns" (paper written for the study of the FECA by the Campaign Finance Study Group of the Institute of Politics, Harvard University, Cambridge, Mass., commissioned by the House Committee on House Administration, 1978).

16. See Henry C. Kenski, "Running with and from the PAC," *Arizona Law Review* 22 (1980): 627–751.

17. Federal Election Commission, *Legislative History of Federal Election Campaign Act of 1974* (Washington, D.C.: U.S. Government Printing Office, 1977), p. 365.

18. Federal Election Commission, *Legislative History of Federal Election Campaign Act of 1976* (Washington, D.C.: U.S. Government Printing Office, 1977), pp. 448–55.

19. For more on the trials of the FEC, see Alexander, *Financing the 1976 Election* (Washington, D.C.: Congressional Quarterly, 1979), chap. 3; and Common Cause, *Stalled from the Start* (Washington, D.C.: Common Cause, 1980). See also *Dollar Politics*, 3rd ed. (Washington, D.C.: Congressional Quarterly, 1982), chap. 2.

20. The Obey-Railsback bill was formally called the Campaign Contribution Reform Act of 1979. It was H.R. 4970, 96th Cong., 1st sess., added to Sen. 832, 125 *Congressional Record*, October 17, 1979, pp. H9303–04.

21. Maxwell Glen, "The PACs Are Back, Richer and Wiser, To Finance the 1980 Elections," *National Journal*, November 24, 1979, pp. 1982–84, reports figures on the numbers of PACs the cutoffs would have affected in 1978, but he apparently uses the $2,500 limit without considering that it becomes a de facto limit of $5,000 in a single cycle of elections.

22. Commentary in Michael J. Malbin, ed., *Parties, Interest Groups, and Campaign Finance Laws* (Washington, D.C.: American Enterprise Institute, 1980), p. 189.

23. For example, see the exchange between Representative Leon

Panetta and Lee Ann Elliott in U.S. Congress, House Committee on House Administration, "Public Financing of Congressional Election," Hearing, 95th Cong., 1st sess., July 21, 1977, pp. 377–78.

24. *Buckley v. Valeo*, 424 U.S. 1 (1976), p. 96.

25. U.S. Congress, House Committee on House Administration, "Public Financing of Congressional Elections," Hearings, 96th Cong., 1st sess., March 15–27, 1979, p. 214.

26. Later a similar bill also lost, 196–213. See Herbert Alexander, *Financing the 1976 Election* (Washington, D.C.: Congressional Quarterly, 1979), pp. 654–60.

27. In Minnesota, for example, in 1980, only two-thirds of the candidates for the legislature in the general election accepted public financing. Almost equal percentages of incumbents and challengers, and of candidates for the Senate and the House, accepted public money. However, many more Democrats accepted than did Republicans; for example, 79 percent of the Democratic candidates for the Senate accepted public financing, but only 42 percent of the Republicans.

28. Gary C. Jacobson, *Money in Congressional Elections* (New Haven: Yale University Press, 1980).

29. Beyond the experience in two presidential elections, there is the experience with public financing in seventeen states, most of which fund state legislative races. See Ruth S. Jones, "State Public Campaign Finances: Implications for Partisan Politics," *American Journal of Political Science* 25 (May 1981): 342–61; and Herbert E. Alexander and Jennifer W. Frutig, *Public Financing of State Elections* (Los Angeles: Citizens' Research Foundation, 1982).

30. On the vouchers, see David Jessup, "Can Political Influence Be Democratized? A Labor Perspective," in *Parties, Interest Groups, and Campaign Finance Laws*, ed. Malbin, pp. 26–55. See also David Adamany and George Agree, *Political Money* (Baltimore: Johns Hopkins University Press, 1975).

31. Bill H.R. 2490 of the first session of the 98th Congress.

32. For support for raising the limits on individual expenditures, see Michael Malbin, "Campaign Financing and the 'Special Interests,'" *Public Interest* 56 (Summer 1979): 21–42.

33. 102 S.Ct. 1266 (1982).

34. *New York Times*, September 3, 1981. The same general idea has more recently been espoused by Mark Green, of the Democracy Project; see the *New York Times*, September 26, 1982.